THE DEBATABLE LAND

A SKETCH OF THE ANGLO-SPANISH
CONTEST FOR THE GEORGIA COUNTRY

Ruins of Santa María Mission, near St. Marys, Georgia.

THE DEBATABLE LAND

A SKETCH OF THE ANGLO-SPANISH
CONTEST FOR THE GEORGIA
COUNTRY

BY

HERBERT E. BOLTON

AND

MARY ROSS

NEW YORK / RUSSELL & RUSSELL

F
289
B73
1968

FIRST PUBLISHED IN 1925
REISSUED, 1968, BY RUSSELL & RUSSELL
A DIVISION OF ATHENEUM HOUSE, INC.
BY ARRANGEMENT WITH THE ESTATE OF HERBERT E. BOLTON
L. C. CATALOG CARD NO: 68-25029
PRINTED IN THE UNITED STATES OF AMERICA

PREFACE

Spain and Portugal effectively and permanently colonized the vast area from Chile to the West Indies and to the Rio Grande—two-thirds of the Western Hemisphere. The late-comers, England, Holland, and France, planted centers of expansion in the left-over areas to the northward. In her northern borderlands Spain's activities were chiefly defensive. Foreign danger there forced her into several salients before she was ready to colonize them. The French intruded into the Caribbean, Florida, Louisiana, and Texas, and border contests ensued. As the English frontier moved westward, the Anglo-Spanish borders overlapped in a succession of areas, and one by one a series of conflicts resulted—in the Caribbean, in Georgia and Florida, in Louisiana, in Texas, in New Mexico, in California. Anglo-American aggression stopped in each case when it reached the line of effective Spanish colonization. Together these border struggles constituted a drama covering two centuries. All the acts had features in common. But each had its own peculiar incidents and characters, and each made its particular contribution to the larger story of American history. One episode in the long contest, brimful of human interest but as yet imperfectly understood, was Spain's resistance to the English in the country that is now Georgia. This is the theme of the historical sketch here presented. The

[v]

PREFACE

survey was written as an introduction to Antonio de Arredondo's *Historical Proof of Spain's Title to Georgia*, just published by the University of California Press. It is here printed separately in the belief that it may interest a wider audience than the one which will welcome the Arredondo document.

Arredondo's *Demostración Historiographica*, as he called his essay, is an interesting and an important document, and its appearance creates a new interest in the early history of the Georgia borderland. It makes clearer than any other work hitherto published the nature of the long contest between Spain and England over the coast region of South Carolina and Georgia. It was written by a trained man who saw service on the disputed frontier as diplomat and soldier. In 1736 Engineer Antonio de Arredondo was sent from Havana to Frederica to protest to Oglethorpe against the establishment of the Georgia colony. In succeeding years he served at intervals in Florida, drawing maps, writing reports, and perfecting the fortifications for the forthcoming struggle with England. In 1742 he was chief-of-staff in the Spanish campaign against Georgia. The *Demostración Historiographica* was dated just before that event, but the narrative terminates somewhat earlier, with the diplomatic contests in 1736–1737. It was written at the request of Güemes y Horcasitas, captain-general of Havana, who directed the Georgia expedition.

The memoir brings into clear relief the following episodes in the early history of the South Atlantic

PREFACE

seaboard: (1) The planting of Spanish settlements on the Georgia-South Carolina coast, 1566–1670. (2) The founding of Charleston in 1670. (3) The treaty of 1670, by which Spain recognized the legality of England's actual settlements in America (including Charleston) at that date. (4) The destruction of the Spanish settlements on the Georgia coast by English and Indian raids, 1670–1702. (5) The founding by Carolinians of Fort King George on the Altamaha in 1721. (6) The diplomatic controversy in America and Europe following thereupon, 1721–1725. (7) The founding of Oglethorpe's Georgia colony, 1733. (8) The resulting diplomatic controversy in America and Europe, 1736–1737 (the Sánchez-Oglethorpe treaty, the Arredondo episode, the Geraldino-Newcastle correspondence).

Arredondo's dissertation was in effect a reply to the English contentions brought forth in the two diplomatic controversies of 1721–1725 and 1736–1737. His argument was essentially this: Spain had first claim to the South Atlantic coast by right of discovery, exploration, and occupation. Between 1566 and 1670 she maintained actual settlements all the way up the Florida-Georgia-South Carolina coast between St. Johns River and Port Royal harbor. They were still occupied when Charleston was founded in 1670. In view of the foregoing, England's claim to the disputed region on the basis of Cabot's voyage, Drake's raid, the Carolina charters, and the Indian grant of Santa Elena (Port Royal) to Dr. Henry Woodward, was baseless and

PREFACE

absurd. By the treaty of 1670 the principle of actual possession was agreed upon by Spain and England; this compact legalized England's ownership as far south as Charleston, and Spain's as far north as Santa Elena Sound, in 32°, 30′ north latitude. Therefore, the subsequent English raids on the Georgia establishments, and all English settlements south of Charleston, were a violation of Spain's rights based on actual settlement, and an infraction of the treaty of 1670.

The editorial Introduction here reproduced is a brief sketch of the ground covered by Arredondo, broadened to include the Georgia back country and extended chronologically to 1763, the time when the Anglo-Spanish contest was ended by the cession of Florida to England. The sketch is the result of extensive independent investigation, based on both manuscript and printed sources. Although more comprehensive, and at many points more explicit, in the main it bears out the soundness of the historical portions of Arredondo's account.

This contribution from the Pacific Coast to the history of the Atlantic Seaboard is a token of the unity of the story of all Spanish North America. In the olden time the Georgia country was one of Spain's Northern Borderlands, linked by common ties with the whole frontier that stretched from the Caribbean westward to the Pacific Ocean. At the very time when Oglethorpe was invading Florida and Vernon was attacking the Isthmus, the Viceroy of New Spain was urging the defensive colonization of Tamaulipas, and taking

PREFACE

measures to protect the California coast and the Manila galleons against capture by George Anson.

My own interest in the early history of the Caribbean area and the "Old Southeast" is one of long standing. In *The Colonization of North America* (Bolton and Marshall), this phase of American history was given new emphasis. Indeed, it was while at work on that book, nearly ten years ago, that I first acquired and used the Arredondo manuscript. In the original draft of *The Spanish Borderlands* there was a chapter on "The Anglo-Spanish Border," which treated briefly the ground covered here in "The Debatable Land," but it was finally cut to a few paragraphs for lack of space, according to the plan of the series in which the book appeared. For several years past, different students in my seminar have studied one or another subject in the field indicated. Three of these especially, Dr. William Edward Dunn, Miss Mary Ross, and Dr. James Guyton Johnson, have brought portions of their work to valuable fruition in published articles or books.

In more recent years there has been a veritable renaissance of interest in the history of the "Old Southeast." Dr. John R. Swanton has made excellent researches in the early history of the Creek Indians; Professor Verner W. Crane is shedding a flood of new light on the southward advance of the English border in the seventeenth and eighteenth centuries; and Dr. Peter H. Guilday is admirably promoting the early Church history of the region. Especially notable is

PREFACE

the work now going on under the direction of the Florida State Historical Society. Through the leadership and the generosity of Mr. John B. Stetson, Jr., and under the scholarly editorial supervision of Dr. James A. Robertson, the Society is proceeding rapidly to the publication of original documents and the preparation of monographs. Notable among the publications thus far completed are Dr. Hrdlicka's *Anthropology of Florida* and Jeannette Thurber Connor's edition of Solís de Merás's *Menéndez de Avilés*.

The preparation of this volume has put me in debt to many persons. First of all must be mentioned Mr. Sidney M. Ehrman, whose generosity and personal interest have made its publication possible. Thanks are due to the administration of the University of California for permission to publish the volume through its press. Especially am I grateful to Mr. Joseph W. Flinn, University Printer, for his great skill and his infinite care in the production of the book. It is a pleasure to acknowledge the valuable aid rendered by Mr. Herbert B. Foster in drafting the maps. For inestimable assistance in the preparation of the text I am indebted to Miss Mary Ross. The actual writing was done by myself, but so great has been her aid that this portion of the work is here published separately under joint-authorship.

HERBERT E. BOLTON.

THE BANCROFT LIBRARY,
UNIVERSITY OF CALIFORNIA,

May 1, 1925.

[x]

CONTENTS

[xi]

LIST OF ILLUSTRATIONS

THE DEBATABLE LAND
A SKETCH OF THE ANGLO-SPANISH
CONTEST FOR THE GEORGIA COUNTRY

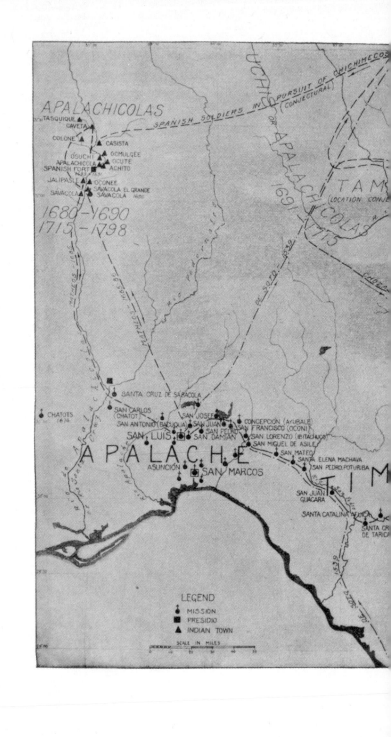

Map of the Georgia Country in Spanish Days.

CHAPTER I

A BIRD'S-EYE VIEW

It is not generally known that for more than a century the Georgia coast was dotted with Spanish missions. But such was the case. From St. Marys River on the south to Port Royal (South Carolina) on the north little centers of Spanish influence were planted in the midst of nearly every coast tribe. Scores of devoted missionaries lived among these children of the forest and taught them the Gospel of Christ. Small soldier garrisons protected the missionaries from their neophytes and guarded the country against the intrusions of unwelcome European neighbors. The Georgia coast constituted the district of Guale, and was a part of the province of La Florida. Most of the Spanish establishments in Guale were on the islands, for these are *terra firma*, while the adjacent mainland presents a wide strip of difficult swamp and salt-marsh, which even yet is unsubdued.

Missionary activity in the Georgia country was not confined to the seaboard. Occasional journeys were made by the friars to the inland tribes. Westward from the Atlantic coast a line of missions stretched along the southern border all the way from Cumberland Island to the lower reaches of the Apalachicola and thence onward to Pensacola. On the banks of the Chattahoochee, near the western fringe of Georgia, a mission was planted in the village of Sábacola. Below the falls of the same stream a presidio was established in the midst of the Apalachicolas, or Lower Creeks.

Spain's principal agents on the Georgia frontier were the missionary and the soldier. The supporting base from which they went forth and by which they were sustained was San Agustín, capital of the province of Florida, of which the Georgia country was a part. Here a presidio served as the center of supply and control, and furnished succor in time of need. The guardian outpost on the north till 1587 was Santa Elena (Port Royal), with its presidio of San Felipe. After Santa Elena was withdrawn, Santa Catalina, near the Savannah, held the border for nearly a century. Spain's main pathways between these outposts were cut through the water. Larger craft braved the storms and waves of the outer sea; smaller vessels sought the shelter of the friendly Inland Passage that winds between the mainland savannahs and the necklace of islands that front the ocean.

The Georgia missions, with their slender garrisons, were not alone signs of Spain's desire to spread the Faith. They were evidences, likewise, of her title to all the vast area included in our "Old Southeast." This title was soon enough contested. From the days of Ribaut and Drake, French and English freebooters almost incessantly came up out of the Caribbean, traded with the natives of the interior, and raided the Spanish settlements on the Atlantic coast. After the founding of Charleston in 1670 the English colonists steadily encroached on the Spanish settlements in Guale, while in the back country the Carolina traders challenged Spain's hold on the Apalachicola Confederacy.

The advantage was with the more aggressive contestant. Step by step the Spanish frontier receded. Santa Elena was first yielded. Then, after a century's actual occupation of the Georgia coast, in 1680 Spain withdrew her Guale outpost from Santa Catalina (St. Catherines) to Zápala and the Altamaha. Six years later, after new raids of Carolinians, Indians, and buccaneers, the frontier retreated to the St. Marys. A decade and a half still later, during Queen Anne's War, it fell back to the St. Johns.

Nor could Spain exclude the English from the hinterland. In vain she sent missionaries to Sábacola; in vain she sent expeditions to capture the traders; in vain she fortified the Chattahoochee. The contest there upset tribal relations and drove the Lower Creeks eastward to the Ocmulgee. Incident to the struggle the Carolinians ruthlessly laid waste thirteen missions in the Tallahasse district that had been continuously occupied by Spain for seventy years.

The Yamassee War (1715) demonstrated the need, long felt, of a buffer English outpost south of the Savannah. The effort to provide it by establishing Fort King George on the Altamaha precipitated a sharp diplomatic controversy. With the coming of Oglethorpe's Georgia colony in 1733 a half decade of bluster and argument followed on that noisy border. The contest for Guale then became part of a larger struggle known as the War of Jenkins' Ear, in which failures were the rule on both sides. The result was indecisive, and Georgia continued to be "debatable land." For a decade or more England nursed the idea of a Neutral Ground, unoccupied by either contestant. She would "make a solitude and call it peace." Hoping thereby to conciliate Spain, she forbade Englishmen to settle south of the Altamaha. But unruly frontiersmen flouted the order and violated the Neutral Ground. In spite of English diplomacy, Spain entered the Seven Years' War, and thereby lost all her lands east of the Mississippi. The century-long contest over the Georgia country was thus ended.

CHAPTER II

THE SPANISH PIONEERS IN GEORGIA AND SOUTH CAROLINA

(1566–1670)

Georgia land, and indeed the whole South Atlantic coast of North America, came into history as a region lying across the pathway to fabled realms of untold wealth and alluring romance. Ayllón, seeking to exploit the land of the Giant King Datha, planted a short-lived colony on the shores of South Carolina (1526). De Soto, in quest of golden Yupaha, and then of enticing Coosa, trod Georgia soil for nearly half a thousand miles. The land failed to yield "gold in quantity," so two decades passed before it was visited once more. The expedition of De Luna and Villafañe sent to plant colonies at Coosa and Santa Elena became the helpless plaything of a hurricane that swept the harbor of Pensacola, where they landed. Discouraged at these costly failures, King Philip II now declared that no further attempt should be made to colonize inhospitable Florida (1561). There were better lands in Mexico and Peru. And so the curtain was rung down on the first act of Georgia and Carolina history.[1]

But Philip's decision was premature. He could not abandon Florida if he would. His words were hardly cold when Frenchmen intruded. Ribaut's ill-starred colony at Port Royal miserably failed (1562). Then Laudonnière planted Fort Caroline on St. Johns River, near the site of Jacksonville (1564). The French menace called for action, and

[1] Early Spanish activities in the southeastern portion of the United States are treated in English by Woodbury Lowery in his two-volume work on *Spanish Settlements Within the Present Limits of the United States, 1513–1574* (New York, 1901, 1905); Bolton, Herbert E., *The Spanish Borderlands* (New Haven, 1921), chs. 1, 3, 5; Shea, J. G., *The Catholic Church in the United States*, vol. I (New York, 1886). Their place in the general history of North America is set forth briefly in Bolton and Marshall, *The Colonization of North America* (New York, 1920), 24, 40–42, 61–65, 253–257. An excellent general account in Spanish is contained in Barcía, Andrés González (Cárdenas), *Ensayo Cronológico para la Historia General de la Florida* (Madrid, 1723). An indication of the original documents for the period before 1543 is given by Hodge and Lewis (editors), *Spanish Explorers in the Southern United States, 1528–1543* (New York, 1907). An interesting account of the expedition of Fray Luís Cancer and that of De Luna and Villafañe is contained in Dávila Padilla, *Historia de la fundación y discurso de la provincia de Santiago de Mexico*, etc. (Brussels, 1625).

Philip sent his ablest seaman to eject the intruders and colonize the threatened coasts. In September, 1565, Menéndez de Avilés reached Florida with a large colony and founded San Agustín. Ten days later he marched stealthily overland, surprised Fort Caroline at dawn, and mercilessly slew most of its defenders.[1]

"Pious cutthroat," Parkman has called Menéndez. But he was more than that. He was a constructive colonizer as well as a hard-fisted soldier. He did not stop with wordy plans; he executed. Within a year he had a line of posts and settlements all the way round the coast from Tampa Bay to Santa Elena (Port Royal).

It was in April, 1566, that the great Adelantado made his first visit to the northern Georgia coast. The chief of Santa Catalina (St. Catherines) Island, where Menéndez

[1] Good accounts of the early French in Florida are given by Lowery, *Spanish Settlements within the present limits of the United States, Florida, 1562–1574*, Bk. I; Parkman, Francis, *The Pioneers of France in the New World;* and Barcía, *Ensayo Cronológico*, 45–46. A briefer sketch is in Bolton, *The Spanish Borderlands*. French accounts are Paul Gaffarel, *Histoire de la Floride Française* (Paris, 1875); Basanier, *Histoire Notable de la Floride* (Paris, 1586), reprinted in Gaffarel, 347–376); Lescarbot, *Histoire de la Nouvelle France* (Paris, 1611).

landed, was an old man called Guale. From this circumstance the name Guale was specifically applied to the island; but it was gradually extended down the entire Georgia coast islands and mainland from Santa Elena to the St. Johns. Landing with fifty men, the Adelantado made friends with old chief Guale, and soon had him sitting on the beach eating biscuits "with gusto." When he departed Menéndez left his nephew and another Spaniard as hostages. On his way back from Santa Elena in August he made another stop of eight days in Guale, and left there a garrison of thirty men. This post on St. Catherines was the first of a chain of Spanish settlements on the Georgia seaboard; its founding in 1566 was the beginning of more than a century's continuous occupation.[1]

[1] Menéndez was not the first Spaniard to visit Guale Island. In 1564 Hernando Manrique de Rojas was sent from Cuba to remove the remains of the colony left at Port Royal by Ribaut. Twelve or fifteen leagues south of Port Royal he visited a town called Guale. It was evidently identical with the Guale visited by Menéndez. The early English settlers of South Carolina used the name Guale for the Georgia coast, spelling it "Wallie," a phonetic equivalent for the Spanish "Guale." The identification of Guale with Amelia Island is correct only after 1686, when the Guale missions were moved southward across the St. Marys. "Lengua de Guale" in the early documents meant, variously, the language, an interpreter, the island, the tongue of land, or the district, of Guale.

While Menéndez hurried up and down the coast, brave Pardo and Boyano explored the back country of Carolina and Georgia. They garnered little or no gold. But they brought back stories of treasure that circulated on the frontier for a century, grew bigger with each passing generation of yarn spinners, and inspired more than one later expedition to the Georgia interior.

Menéndez was a soldier of God as well as of the King. So he brought Jesuit missionaries to teach the natives Christianity and the elements of European civilization. Brothers Domingo Agustín and Pedro Ruíz led the way to Guale (1568). Three others soon followed. Brother Domingo was a born linguist, and within six months he had translated the Catechism and prepared a grammar in the Yamassee tongue. This Guale grammar, it would seem, was the first ever written on United States soil. But Brother Domingo wrote no more grammars in this world. Before the end of the year he died during an epidemic, a martyr to the Faith in Georgia. Father Rogel went to Orista, near Port Royal, or Santa Elena. On the southern end of the Georgia littoral Menéndez established another garrison called San Pedro. It was soon followed by a mission. These first Jesuit missionary labors were short lived. The Indians had their own view of things. During an uprising in 1570 the missions of Guale and Orista were deserted. Father Segura and his little band withdrew to Virginia, where they were forthwith slaughtered by the very Indians they hoped to save. At the same time the garrisons at San Agustín, San Pedro, and San Felipe were reduced to fifty men each.

The Jesuits had gone; Menéndez soon followed them.[1] For seven years La Florida had been the great man's chief care. In 1572

[1] The work of Menéndez de Avilés is sketched in Lowery's second volume, *Florida, 1562–1574.* The book is sound. Although Parkman (*Pioneers of France in the New World*) is unsympathetic toward the Spaniards, his sketch of Menéndez's career possesses literary qualities lacked by that of Lowery, and is still valuable. A contemporary account is the *Memorial que hizo el Doctor Gonzalo Solís de Merás, de todas las jornadas y sucesos del Adelantado Pedro Menéndez de Avilés.* It was published in Spanish by Ruidíaz y Caravia in his *La Florida, su conquista y colonización por Pedro Menéndez de Avilés* (Madrid, 1893). Just recently an excellent English translation of Merás has been made by Jeannette Thurber Connor and published under the title of *Pedro Menéndez de Avilés* (Deland, 1923). Ruidíaz gives a good sketch of Menéndez's life, ample bibliographies, and extensive documentary appendices. His book is fundamental for the early history of the Atlantic coast. Barcía's *Ensayo Cronológico* contains a good general account. Other contemporary accounts are in Genaro García (ed.), *Dos Antiguas Relaciones de la Florida* (Mexico, 1902). Data concerning Father Rogel will be found in the *Historical Magazine,* vol. V, pp. 327–330 (New York, 1861).

he left it never to return. Now for the greater part of two decades the fortunes of the province were directed by his able nephew, Pedro Menéndez Marqués. Among his manifold difficulties Indian uprisings in Santa Elena and Guale were not the least. A Christian chief was killed in Guale. Solís, commander at Santa Elena, posted down the Inland Passage and hanged some of the offenders. When their chance came, the Gualeans repaid the compliment by massacring nine Spaniards at Espogache, a village near the Altamaha.[1] Among the slain was Pedro Menéndez, the Crosseyed, another nephew of the Adelantado.

These Indian disturbances were encouraged by French corsairs who harried the coast, for other Gauls had followed in the wake of Ribaut. They traded profitably in sassafras, and they intrigued with the Indians. But

[1] The rebellion at Santa Elena in 1576 and the raids of Estrozi and Gil are treated by Mary Ross of the University of California in her "French Intrusions and Indian Uprisings in Georgia and South Carolina, 1577–1580" (*Georgia Historical Quarterly*, Vol. VII, no. 3, September 1923, pp. 251–281). The wealth of materials for this period in the Archivo General de Indias is indicated by the footnotes to Miss Ross's article. A description of the new fort built at Santa Elena after the uprising of 1576 is given by Flores in his manuscript report made in 1578 (A. G. I., 2–5–2/10). A later French intrusion is treated by Miss Ross in "The French on the Savannah, 1605" (*Georgia Historical Quarterly*, Vol. VIII, no. 3, September, 1924, pp. 167–194).

some of them paid dearly for their ventures.
One such was Estrozi, head of one of these
marauding bands. He was captured by
Marqués in Guale, taken to San Agustín,
questioned, and then summarily executed with
twenty-two of his men (1579). In the following summer no less than twenty French
corsair vessels were seen on the Georgia coast.
Their leader, Captain Gil, was slain in a hot-
fought battle in San Juan River. Marqués
now had a breathing spell. But these were not
the last of the sassafras gatherers.

Such a frontier demanded more missionaries, and the place of the Jesuits was taken
by the Franciscans. These "precursors" began
a work in Georgia which lasted for a century—
and was then forgotten.[1] The first band of

[1] Most of the records of the work of the first Franciscans in
the Georgia country are still in manuscript. Many of these are
contained in the Archivo General de Indias. Barcía (*Ensayo
Cronológico*) gives valuable data. Torquemada, *Monarquía
Indiana* (Madrid, 1723), Ch. XXX, gives a detailed account of
the uprising of the Guale Indians, which occurred shortly before
he wrote. This book was first printed in Seville in 1615. In
modern times pioneer work of high character was done by John
Gilmary Shea, in his *Catholic Church in the United States*, vol. I.
Shea was followed closely by Rev. Father Zephyrin Engelhardt
in a series of valuable articles published in the *Franciscan Herald*,
vols. I-III (1913–1915). More recently J. G. Johnson has published *The Spanish Period of Georgia and South Carolina, 1566–
1702* (Bulletin of the University of Georgia, May, 1923).

the Little Brothers came to Santa Elena in
1573. Most of their work centered around
San Agustín. Part of them went to Guale
only to be driven out or slain. But the friars
held on. Churches were built in the principal
towns—at Tolomato, at Tupique, at Guale,
at Yoa. On the southern coast San Pedro
(Cumberland Island) became an important
missionary center, where Father Baltasar
López won fame. But the hero of all this early
Franciscan period was Fray Alonso Reynoso.
Devout, gentle, zealous, tireless, his figure,
though shadowy in the distance, still looms
large and strong. He was a sixteenth century
Serra on the Atlantic coast.[1]

[1] Father Reynoso's work is dealt with in a Council warrant,
Madrid, November 12, 1583; royal cédula to the Casa de Contratación, November 22, 1583; to Fray Alonso de Reynoso,
March 31, 1584; to the Casa de Contratación, February 3, 1587;
to the same, February 23, 1587; to the royal officials of Florida,
October 11, 1589; to the same, October 18, 1589; the Council of
the Indies to Antonio de Cartagena, November 6, 1589; royal
cédula to the officials of Florida, March 17, 1587; to the Casa de
Contratación, June 1, 1587; to the same, September 20, 1589;
to the governor of Florida, March 6, 1590 (all the foregoing are
in A. G. I., 154–1–18). In a letter dated at San Agustín, May 10,
1586, Governor Marqués wrote in highest praise of the friar.
"I can tell your Majesty that he has worked hard among these
people, for since he came he has never left them." (A. G. I.,
54–5–16, Doc. no. 48.) His work is reviewed in a document of
1602 entitled Florida, Materias Gubernativas (A. G. I., 86–5–24).

Guale's importance was increased by Drake's attack, for that bold raid caused the removal of the Santa Elena garrison to San Agustín (1587). Santa Catalina, the mission near the Savannah, was now the northern outpost. A new epoch was opened in 1595, when, in the cool of October, Governor Avendaño conducted five more friars to Guale. Gratifying success attended their labors. In seven towns along the Georgia coast old churches were restored or new ones built.[1] Father Chozas the explorer, and Pareja the linguist, labored on San Pedro Island; Dávila, the captive-to-be, on Ospo (Jekyl); Velascola the Cantabrian giant, on Asao (St. Simons); the veteran Corpa on the mainland at Tolomato, across from Zápala (Sapelo) Island; Rodríguez at Tupique three leagues north, and also on the mainland; Auñon and Badajoz at Santa Catalina. Encouraged by bountiful harvests on the coast, Fathers Chozas and Velascola journeyed inland eight days on horseback to

[1] An illuminating report of the missions in 1597 is given in Ynformación hecha en S. Agustín de la Florida ante fray Francisco Marron, custodio cura y vicario de aquellas Provincias, sobre la pobreza y necesidad en que se encuentran los Religiosos Misioneros y del buen efecto de las misiones entre los naturales. January 23, 1597 (A. G. I., 54–5–20).

distant Tama and Ocute, Creek towns near the upper Altamaha. Their enthusiastic reports revived old tales of Boyano's Diamond Mountain, and stirred up new dreams of interior conquest.

For two years the Guale missions flourished. Then suddenly the thunderbolt of rebellion came out of a clear sky. Juan, a heady young chief, heir of the mico of Tolomato, organized a conspiracy. Followers were not hard to find, and in September, 1597, the blow fell.[1] Father Corpa was slain and beheaded. From Tolomato the angry mob rushed to the other missions, gathering strength as it went. The tide first turned north and then it surged southward. Father Rodríguez at Tupique, Auñon and Badajoz at Santa Catalina, and Velascola at Asao, suffered a fate like that of Father Corpa. Father Dávila at Ospo was wounded, seized,

[1] The story of the Guale revolt is set forth at some length by Torquemada in his *Monarquía Indiana*, which was written shortly after the event. Barcía (Cárdenas) retold the story a century and a quarter later in his *Ensayo Cronológico*. Accounts in English are given by Shea (*The Catholic Church in the United States*, I); Engelhardt (*Franciscan Herald*, vol. I), and Johnson, J. G. ("The Yamassee Revolt of 1597 and the Destruction of the Georgia Missions," *Georgia Historical Quarterly*, vol. VII, pp. 44–53, March, 1923).

Santa Catalina Island, looking south, down the Inland Passage.

and carried into a captivity that was worse than death. But the Indians at San Pedro remained faithful, and there the bloody massacre spent its force.

A hurried appeal for help was sent from San Pedro to San Agustín. To punish the offenders Governor Canzo arose from a sick bed and sailed north up the Inland Passage with a hundred and fifty soldiers. The Indians everywhere fled in terror.[1] At Ospo, Zápala, Tolomato, Guale, Tupique, Asao, and Talaje, Canzo destroyed all that was left of towns and cornfields. But he could find no Indians to chastize. Other punitive expeditions were made, and the Indians at last submitted. After nearly a year Father Dávila was recovered from captivity. Don Lucas, a young

[1] Manuscript materials for the history of the subjugation of the Indians are voluminous. Some of the documents are the following: Carta del Gobernador de la Florida Gonzalo Mendez de Canço á S. M. San Agustín, February 23, 1598 (A. G. I., 54–5–9); Ynformación sobre la muerte de los Relixiosos, July 11, 1598 (A. G. I., Patronato, 1–1–1/19 Ro. 28);Carta de Gonzalo Mendez de Canço, Gobernador de la Florida, á S. M. En ella trata de la muerte que dieron los Yndios de guale á los Religiosos, San Agustín, August 8, 1598; Auto y pregon del Gobernador de la Florida Gonsalo Mendes de Canço, sobre la libertad de los Yndios, January 31, 1600; Testimonio cerca de la pacificacion de los caciques de la provincia de Guale. May 18, 1600 (A. G. I., 54–5–9).

hostage who confessed to a part in the uprising, was hanged at San Agustín on the public scaffold. The harsh punishment had its effect. Now the Guale chiefs renewed their allegiance, were granted pardon, and once more loyally furnished levies of laborers for the public works at San Agustín.

The restoration of the missions followed. They were urgently needed. The coast demanded protection against a new swarm of French corsairs. The interior beckoned. Canzo projected a colony at Tama, and sent Juan de Lara inland nine days to investigate rumors of strangers.[1] To prepare the way for missionaries, Ibarra the new governor, made a triumphal visit to the Guale towns. There was another year of waiting, then seven more sandaled friars reached San Agustín. Early in 1606 part of them were escorted north up the Inland Passage. The destroyed churches had already been rebuilt, and the friars were welcomed with ceremony. Once more the

[1] Ideas concerning the interior, and plans for interior expansion, are set forth in Ynformacion hecha de oficio ante Don Gonzalo Mendez de Canço, Gobernador de las Provincias de la Florida, sobre la situation de la Tama y sus riquezas y de la poblacion de Yngleses. San Agustín, February 4, 1600; Carta del Gover.or de la Florida, 22 Sep.e 1602 (A. G. I., 54–5–9); Florida, Materias Gubernativas, 1602 (A. G. I., 86–5–24).

Georgia forests echoed the peaceful tones of
the Angelus bell. Father Juan de Capillas
took charge at San Pedro; Pedro Delgado at
Talaje and Espogache; Pedro Ruíz at Santa
Catalina. What these Brown Robes had accomplished by summer is revealed in the
report by the bishop of Cuba, who then made
the first pastoral visit ever accomplished on
United States soil. At the four Georgia
missions he confirmed 1070 neophytes. Guale
had come back to the Christian fold.[1]

Activity in the Georgia missions was
stimulated by a new cloud in the northern
sky. In the very year after the Franciscans
returned to Guale the English settled at
Jamestown. Philip III might easily have
crushed the weak little post, but he tempor-

[1] The manuscript materials for the restoration of friendly
relations with Guale and the reestablishment of the missions are
extensive. The following are some of them: Visita hecha por
el Gouᵒʳ. Gᵒ. Mendez de Canzo, February, 1603; Carta del
Gouer.ᵒʳ de la Florida G.ᵒ Mendez de Canço, 15 de Abril, 603;
Discurso del uiaje que ba a hacer el Señor Pedro de Ybarra . . .
November, 1604; Opinion of Juan Maldonado Barnuevo, Valla-
dolid, March 21, 1605 (A. G. I., 54–5–9); Carta de Pedro de
Ybarra al padre Benito Blasco, San Agustín, December 7, 1605;
Testimonio de una carta de Pedro de Ybarra al Padre Fray
Vermejo, December 13, 1605 (A. G. I., 54–5–17); Relacion
presentada a S. M. en su Consejo de Yndias, June 26, 1606
(A. G. I., 54–5–20); Ybarra to the King, June 26, 1606 (A. G. I.,
54–5–9).

ized, misled by his advisors to think that the struggling colony would fail through disease and starvation. Nevertheless, the danger set in motion a new wave of missionary activity. Indeed, the seventeenth century was the Golden Age of the Franciscans in the "Old Southeast." Their work was at once a crusade against heathendom and a defensive move to hold the border.[1] In 1612 the Atlantic coast was included in a new missionary province called Santa Elena, and Fray Juan de Capillas, the Georgia missionary, went to live at Havana as first provincial. New friars came in large numbers. Fray Luís de Ore, "gran teólogo," arrived with twenty-four workers in 1612. All through the century others followed at frequent intervals. Thirty, forty, or even fifty at a time was the usual corps in the Florida province, of which Guale was a part. Baptisms were sometimes stimulated by epidemics; at other times they were

[1] For Spain's reaction to Virginia, see Brown, Alexander, *Genesis of the United States* (Boston, 1890), I, 115–127, and elsewhere; Brown, Alexander, *The First Republic in America* (Boston, 1898), 91; Irene A. Wright, "Spanish Policy toward Virginia" (*American Historical Review*, April, 1920, 448, *et seq.*); *Calendar of State Papers, Colonial, America and the West Indies* (London, 1860–1910), 1675–78, pp. 45 *et seq.* See also the following manuscripts: Carta incompleta de Pedro de Ibarra,

retarded by lack of funds. The friars continued to make occasional visits to Tama in the interior, and by the middle of the century they had returned to Santa Elena (Port Royal).

Of the missions on the coast we have a picture drawn in 1655. Five of them were within the present Georgia. These were San Pedro on Cumberland Island; San Buenaventura on St. Simons Island; Santo Domingo at Talaje, on the mainland; San José on Sapelo Island; and Santa Catalina on St. Catherines Island. Beyond the Savannah, in South Carolina, there were San Felipe on Parris Island, and Chatuache, six leagues farther north.

Varied indeed were the labors of these pioneers of Georgia and South Carolina. At the missions there were churches and houses to build, fields to clear, and the monotonous round of spiritual offices to perform. There

January 4, 1608 (A. G. I., 54–5–9); Royal cédula to Pedro de Ybarra, "sobre que haga descubrir las bayas y puertos que ay en la Virginia." El Pardo, November 8, 1608 (A. G. I., 87–5–2); Alonso de las Alas to the King, San Agustín, November 23, 1609 (A. G. I., 56–5–14); Orden del Gobernador D. Pedro de Ybarra (de S. Agustín de la Florida) a el Capitan Francisco Fernandez de Ecija para reconocer las costas del norte (A. G. I., Patronato 2–5–3/16); Derrotero que hizo Andres Gonzales al Xacan (A. G. I., Patronato 1–1–1/19 Rº. 31).

were children to instruct, daily masses to be sung, and special ceremonies to be performed on feast days; there were marriages to solemnize, babes to baptize, medical aid to administer to the sick, and last rites to perform for the dying and the dead. All these activities must be carefully written down as a matter of record.[1] This, too, was faithfully done, for models of neatness are the old mission books. But these routine labors were only part of the missionary's toil. He must write long letters to his religious superiors or to the governor at

[1] Data concerning Father Ore's friars is given in Barcía, *Ensayo Cronológico*, 181–184. Missionary progress is revealed in Carta a S. M. de Varios Religiosos, January 17, 1617; Carta del Provincial y definidores, January 24, 1617; Carta de Fray Juan de Santander, November 25, 1630 (A. G. I., 54–5–20); Copia de carta que Luís de Horruytiner escrivio a Su Magestad, November 15, 1633 (A. G. I., 54–5–10); Barcía, *op. cit.*, 197; Shea, *The Catholic Church in the United States*, I, 162–5; Carta para S. M. de Fray Francisco Alonso de Jesus, February 7, 1635; Gov. Ruíz to the King, April 16, 1645 (A. G. I., 54–5–10); Memoria de las Poblaciones, MS. cited by Shea, *op. cit.*, p. 166; Consulta del consejo, July 28, 1646 (A. G. I., 54–5–20); Barcía, *op. cit.*, 212; Father Pérez, Memorial para S. M., July 28, 1646; Memorial of Fray Pedro Moreno Ponce de León, July 21, 1648; Memorial of Fray Pedro Moreno Ponce de León, September 7, 1651; Petition of Guale Indians, October 17, 1657 (A. G. I., 54–5–20). Rebolledo to the king, October 18, 1657 (in Brooks, A., *Unwritten History of Old St. Augustine* (St. Augustine, 1909?), 102–105). Relación de los Religiosos, July 8, 1658 (A. G. I., 54–5–20); the governor to the king, August 6, 1668 (A. G. I., 54–5–9).

San Agustín. He must report all disturbances among the Indians, or rumors of intruding Englishmen; for these missionaries were news-agents and diplomats on the frontier, as well as spiritual teachers.

Missions were not solely a matter of friars and soldier guards. The Indian was the central figure; and he was not always happy. He was between two masters, the secular and the spiritual arms of the state. Sometimes he complained. Sometimes he was able to make his voice heard—not always. His complaints were quite as likely to be echoes of the wranglings of friar and official as of the yearnings of the neophyte for a happier lot.[1] In rare instances, as had been the case in 1597, he broke out in open revolt.

The shadow of Jamestown soon projected itself into the Carolina-Georgia back country.

[1] Los Religiosos de San Francisco Fr. Sebastían Martínez, Fr. Carlos de Anguiano y Fr. Gabriel Fernández, a S. M., Guale, Noviembre 8, 1657. They transmit a complaint of the Guale Indians dated October 16, 1657 (A. G. I., 54-5-20); Dictamen fiscal, Madrid, May 24, 1660; Governor Alonso de Aranguíz y Cotes to the king, November 15, 1661 (El Gobernador de la Florida informa á S. M. contestando a una Real Cédula, sobre lo que pidió Santiago, Mico de Tolomato, y otros principales, cerca de que los Gobernadores, les occupaban en servicios personales, etc. (A. G. I., 54-5-10).

Ever since the days of the Roanoke colony the English settlers had talked of Spanish mines and west flowing rivers in the interior. These loadstones of adventure lured Englishman as well as Spaniard. Loquacious John Smith led the way to the falls of the James. Other Anglomen unknown to history soon followed his track and lengthened it toward the Spanish border.[1] Echoes of their movements reached Spanish circles, where a little fact got sadly mixed with much imagination. Guale Indians reported strange men on horseback, and ruddy faced foreigners who found favor with the Indian women. Fear of foreign intrusion was intertwined with an ever recurrent desire to seek the pearls of Cufitachiqui, or Boyano's Diamond Mountain.

From time to time, in the course of the seventeenth century, Spanish expeditions were sent to investigate these rumors. Soldiers and Indians despatched by Governor Salinas in 1624 scoured the Georgia-Carolina interior for

[1] For English activities see: Peter Force, *Tracts and Other Paper Relating principally to the Origin, Settlement, and Progress of the Colonies in North America*, III, no. 11, p. 15 (Washington, 1844); Alvord and Bidgood, *The First Explorations of the Trans-Allegheny Region by the Virginians, 1650–1674* (Cleveland, 1912), 103, 104.

Another view of the ruins of Santa María Mission,
near St. Marys, Georgia.

one hundred and fifty leagues, but they found no trace of the rumored "gente blanca á caballo." Another party sent by Salinas had like success. A little later Pedro de Torres, ten soldiers, and sixty Guale Indians traveled four months in the back country of Georgia and Carolina, and covered two hundred leagues (1628). They, too, failed to find Englishmen. Rumors of fair-haired strangers continued to come, and in 1661 a Spanish expedition was made all the way across Georgia to the Apalachicolas, or Lower Creeks.[1]

During these years things were happening on the southern fringes of Georgia. The old Timucua missions reached northward to minister to the Indians in the region where Statenville and Valdosta now stand. The center of a new movement was Apalache, with San Luís (now Tallahassee) as its focus. Toward this important region in the back

[1] Luis de Rojas y Borja to the king, January 20, 1625; the king to Rojas, May 3, 1627; Carta de Don Luís de Rojas y Borja, Governador de la Florida á Su Magestad. Trata en ella de un descubrimiento de perlas hecho en Cofitachiqui. San Agustín, June 30, 1628; El Gobernador de la florida, D. Alonso de Aranguíz y Cotes a S. M., Florida, Septiembre 8, de 1662 (A. G. I., 54–5–10); El Alférez Juan Bauptista Terrazas a Su Magestad, ca. 1682, with decree of October 6, 1682 (A. G. I., 54–5–19 No. 50).

country French and English pirates on the
Gulf, empty flour barrels at San Agustín, and
the demand of the royal fleets for wild turkeys
pointed the finger of prophecy.   The Apalache
Indians had long been asking for missionaries,
but for lack of funds and workers the petition
could not be answered till 1633.   Then the
guardian of the head monastery at San
Agustín trudged westward and answered the
call.   Twenty years later there were nine
flourishing missions in Apalache, all within a
few leagues of the principal mission at San
Luís.   Some of them drew neophytes from the
region that is now southwestern Georgia.

Missionary work carried with it other
developments toward civilization in western
Florida.   A garrison was stationed at San
Luís.   Packet boats soon plied between San
Agustín, Havana, and San Marcos Bay (1639).
Apalache became a lively center for trade in
deerskins and wild turkeys.   Of maize and
beans three or four thousand bushels were
shipped annually to San Agustín.   At Asile
(Aucilla) a royal plantation was opened.
Hostile Choctaws in the west, pirates on the
Gulf, and English traders in the back country
increased the importance of Apalache.   The

military defence was strengthened, and San Luís became a base for advance toward Pensacola and up the Chattahoochee into western Georgia.[1]

[1] Manuscript materials for the history of the Tallahassee district in the seventeenth century are plentiful. The following are a few: Fray Francisco Al° de Jhs. á Su Magestad, Florida. Sin fecha, with Decreto 27 de Febrero de 1635; D. Luís Horruytiner, á S. M., S. Agustín. Junio 24, 1637; Same to same, September 12, 1638; Parrafos de una carta de Damian de Vega, August 22, 1639 (A. G. I., 54–5–10); Francisco Menéndez Marqués y Pedro Benedit Horruytiner, a S. M. July 27, 1647 (A. G. I., 54–5–20. Doc. no. 50); El Rey a Oficiales reales, Balzain, 24 Octubre, 1653 (A. G. I., 54–5–11); Memoria de las Poblaciones, 1655 (cited by Shea, op. cit., I, 165–166); Carta de Fray Juan Gomez de Engraba, Havana, March 13, 1657 (A. G. I., 54–5–10. Doc. no. 73); Memorial of friars Francisco de San Antonio, Juan de Medina, Sebastián Martínez, Jacinto Domínguez, Alonso del Moral, and Juan Caldera, to his Majesty, Florida, September 10, 1657; Carta de los Religiosos de la Provincia de Santa Elena a S. M., September 10, 1657 (A. G. I., 54–5–20); Carta de los Religiosos de la Florida, June 16, 1664 (A. G. I., 54–5–18).

CHAPTER III

THE ANGLO-SPANISH CONTEST FOR GUALE
(1670–1686)

A new menace now arose in the north. The English came up out of the Caribbean to settle on the very soil of old Santa Elena, next door to Santa Catalina. The impulse for the settlement of South Carolina came from the Antilles. Plantations there were playing out; new lands were needed; a "westward movement" to the mainland resulted. Sir John Colleton, Barbadian planter, interested a group of men in the Carolina country. A charter granted to eight Proprietors all the region from 36° to 31°. Two years later the paper boundaries were pushed south to 29°. Who cared that Spain at that very moment had, within the area granted, a line of settlements stretching up the coast for one hundred and fifty miles, some of them nearly a century old? Or that the grant included El Paso and Santa Fé?

William Hilton was sent from Barbados to explore the Carolina coast. When he arrived at Parris Island he found there Captain Argüelles with soldiers from San Agustín. Presents were exchanged. The Spaniards proffered venison and pork; the Englishmen responded with a jug of brandy. But Hilton was cautious and withdrew to avoid capture. The Spaniards had blocked the way to Port Royal.[1]

Three years later Yeamans, one of the Proprietors, took a colony to Cape Fear River. Then, while he returned to Barbados, Robert Sandford sailed south to explore. With him went young Dr. Henry Woodward, a man of destiny on that international border. Santa Elena was Sandford's goal. No Span-

[1] For Hilton, Yeamans, Sandford, and Woodward, see *Shaftesbury Papers* (South Carolina Historical Society Collections, Vol. V, 1897), pp. 18–28, 57–82, and index; McCrady, Edward, *The History of South Carolina under the Proprietary Government, 1670–1719* (New York, 1897), pp. 71–72, 81–93; *Calendar of State Papers, Colonial, America and West Indies, 1669–1674* (London, 1889), p. 246; Swanton, J. R., *Early History of the Creek Indians* (Washington, 1922), 62–67. For a biographical sketch of Woodward, see Joseph W. Barnwell, "Dr. Henry Woodward, The First English Settler in South Carolina, and Some of his Descendants (*South Carolina Historical and Genealogical Magazine*, VIII, no. 1, January, 1907, pp. 29–41). Among Woodward's many distinguished descendants one was Robert Y. Hayne, of "Webster-Hayne debate" fame.

iards were there now, but "a faire woodden
Crosse of the Spaniards ereccon" stood in the
plaza of the town on Parris Island, and signs of
preparation for new buildings were in sight.
When on July 8 Sandford departed he took
with him the nephew of the cacique of Santa
Elena; in his place he left Dr. Woodward.   A
formal ceremony sealed the arrangement.
The whole village being assembled, Sandford
delivered Woodward into the keeping of the
head chiefs and their wives.   Woodward was
placed beside the cacique on a throne, given
the cacique's niece for a housekeeper, and
endowed by the Niquesalla with "formall possession of the whole Country to hold as
Tennant at Will of the right Hono^ble Lords
Proprietors."[1]

A site for a colony had been selected.   But
it was debatable ground, destined to witness
stirring scenes.   Twenty years of conflict
were necessary to decide the possession of
Santa Elena.   Spaniard, Indian, and Scotch-
man, each lent color to the moving picture

[1] For the failure of the Cape Fear settlement and the founding
of Charleston, see *Shaftesbury Papers,* 13, 25, 31, 52, 89, 93, 130,
136, 141–143, 158, 161, 163, 168, 178, 217–218, 263, 273; McCrady
Carolina Under the Proprietary Government, chs. 3–5; Carroll,
Historical Collections of South Carolina, I, ch. 2 (New York, 1836).

staged on its shores.   The key to the border
was in the pocket of Dr. Henry Woodward.
He studied the country and learned the
tongues of the natives.   Months were spent
in these pursuits, then Spaniards carried him
to San Agustín.   The English account has it
that he was captured.   The Spanish version
is that he went of his own accord.   Be that
as it may, at San Agustín he found favor.   He
lived with the parish priest, became a Catholic,
and was made official surgeon.   Thus ad-
vantaged, he learned the secrets of the country
and then awaited a chance to escape.   It soon
came.   In 1668 the freebooter, Robert Searles,
favored Florida with a visit.[1]   By a mirth
provoking trick he entered the harbor at San
Agustín and ransacked the town.   In the
confusion Woodward fled to the English and
with them sailed to the Antilles.   Within two

[1] For the Searles attack on San Agustín in 1668 and the
escape of Woodward see Carta del Licenciado francisco Sotolongo,
Cura de la Yglesia de aquella Provincia de la Florida, San
Agustín, July 4, 1668 (A. G. I., 54–5–20); Carta de Juan Menéndez
Marquéz, July 4, 1668; Carta del capitan Antonio de Agüelles,
July 6, 1668 (A. G. I., 54–5–18); Governor Francisco de la
Guerra y de la Vega to the queen, San Agustín, August 6, 1668
(A. G. I., 54–5–9); Carta de D. Nicolas Ponce de Leon á la reyna
August 6, 1668; Carta de D. francisco de la Guerra y de la Vega,
August 8, 1668 (A. G. I., 54–5–18).

years he was back in South Carolina, and
ready once more to annoy the Spaniards.

Cayagua harbor and not Port Royal was
now chosen for the seat of a colony, and there
in 1670 Kiawah (Charlestown, Charleston)
was founded. The Spaniards called it San
Jorge. A few weeks later England's right to
Charleston was legalized by a treaty which
adopted the principle of actual occupation.[1]
By it Spain recognized all English settlements
then established, but no others.

The English colonists found themselves, as
they complained, "in the very chaps of the
Spaniards." And they soon felt their teeth.
One of the vessels bound for Charleston by
accident made anchor at Mission Santa Catalina, near the Savannah. The English were
treated as invaders. In a skirmish several of
the passengers were killed, and by a trick
John Rivers and William Carr were captured.
Governor Sayle at Charleston sent a rescue

[1] For the treaty of 1670, see Chalmers, *A Collection of Treaties*
(London, 1790), II, 35; Calvo, *Colección Completa de Tratados*
(Paris, 1862), I, 162; Herstlet, *A Complete collection of Treaties
and Conventions* (London, 1840), vol. II. Haring, *The Buccaneers
in the West Indies in the XVII Century* (New York, 1910), 196–
197; 200, 209; Harris, F. R., *Life of Edward Montagu, First Earl
of Sandwich, 1625–1672* (London, 1912), 84–109; 209–210;
Stevens, *History of Georgia* (New York, 1847, Philadelphia, 1859),
I, 141.

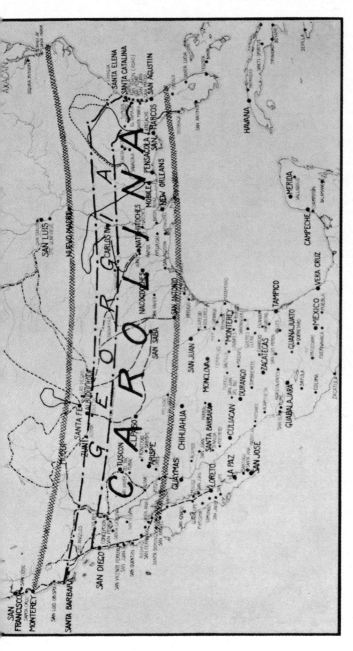

Map of the Carolina Grant of 1665 and of the Georgia Grant of 1732, superimposed on a map of the northern Spanish frontier.

expedition with a blustering threat. Joseph Bailey and John Collins carried the message from the sloop to the mission. They, in turn, were captured, and like Rivers and Carr, were sent prisoners to San Agustín.[1]

Governor Guerra was alarmed. Here was serious business, indeed. Stay at San Jorge the English must not, for they were on Spanish soil. So three frigates were equipped and put under command of Juan Menéndez Marqués. Fourteen pirogues rowed by Indians accompanied the ships. When on August 18 the crimson and gold waved off Cayagua harbor there seemed little hope for San Jorge. But the mighty Atlantic intervened to protect

[1] For the capture of Rivers, Carr, Bailey, and Collins and their experience at San Agustín, see *Shaftesbury Papers*, 135, 169, 170, 199, and index; W. E. Dunn, "Letter from Joseph Baily," December 12, 1672 (*South Carolina Historical and Genealogical Magazine*, XVIII, pp. 54–56, no. 1, January, 1917. See below); *Colonial Records of North Carolina*, I, 207 (Raleigh, 1886); McCrady, *op. cit.*, 126–129; Declaraciones de los Yngleses, San Agustín, October, 1671 (A. G. I., 58–1–26); Governor Manuel de Zendoya to the crown, March 24, 1672 (A. G. I., 54–5–11); Joseph Bailey to the ambassador from England to Spain, San Agustín, December 12, 1672; filed with the original English letter is a Spanish translation (A. G. I., 58–1–26); Certificación sobre defuncion del Ingles D. Juan de Rivera, San Agustín, March 8, 1675 (A. G. I., 54–5–11); Salazar to the crown, January 20, 1677; Salazar to the crown, March 6, 1680, enclosing declarations of five English prisoners at San Agustín (A. G. I., 58–1–26).

the infant colony.   A heavy sea carried away the cables of the Spanish frigates and they withdrew to San Agustín.[1]

Charleston was safe for the moment.   But for years the settlers lived in dread.   Indian disturbances were charged to Spanish complicity.   The danger was increased by runaway white servants and negro slaves.   Fear was mingled with anger.[2]   Then arose the cry that "Wallie" with its hated missions must be destroyed.   Destroyed they were in due time.

The English intrusion, coupled with fierce pirate raids, stimulated a Spanish program of defense.   At Santa Catalina a garrison was now established beside the mission.   It was the founding of Charleston that introduced the stone age at San Agustín.   Hitherto the old fort had been a wooden structure.   But now a crisis had arisen.   Funds were appro-

[1] The expedition of Marqués against Charleston is briefly treated in Echagaray's Memorial, 1684, paragraph 1 (A. G. I., 61–6–20); Report of Guerra, Madrid, July 12, 1673 (A. G. I., 58–1–26); see also *Shaftesbury Papers*, 178, 194, 198–199; McCrady, *Carolina under the Proprietary Government*, 130; Carroll, B. R., *Historical Collections of South Carolina*, II, 370 (New York, 1836).

[2] Uneasiness at Charleston over the Spanish border in 1671–1672 is reflected in the *Journal of the Grand Council of South Carolina*, August 25, 1671–June 24, 1680 (edited by A. S. Salley, Jr.), pp. 8–9, 14, 22, 45.

priated, stone was quarried, lime kilns were opened, and an engineer and artisans brought from Havana. Indians were levied from Guale, Timucua, and Apalache to work on the fortification.[1] Sleepy old San Agustín was stirred to new life. Delays occurred, but when Quiroga came (1687) as governor he found "completed in the main" the great castle which still stands at San Agustín, a monument to Spain's determination.[2]

For a decade the English cloud hovered over Santa Catalina, guardian of the Guale

[1] Defensive measures in Guale and San Agustín are treated in two letters of Governor Ponce de León to the queen, July 8, 1673 (A. G. I., 58-1-26); an undated summary of defensive efforts, *ca.* 1675, in Brooks, *The Unwritten History of Old St. Augustine*, pp. 130–135; Zendoya to the king, December 15, 1672 (*Ibid.*, 115–117); Carta del Comisario general de indias sobre los religiosos que asisten en la provincia de Santa Helena de la Florida, May 2, 1673 (A. G. I., 54-5-20); Salazar to the king, June 15, 1675 (Brooks, *op. cit.*, 125–129); Salazar to the king, August 23, 1675 (Brooks, *op. cit.*, 121–123); to the sovereign, November 23, 1675 (Brooks, *op. cit.*, 123–125); Quiroga to the king, December 20, 1687 (A. G. I., 2-4-1/19, no. 17).

[2] Defensive measures at Apalache during the same period are discussed in Salazar to the queen, June 15, 1675 (A. G. I., 54-5-11); Salazar to the king, September 6, 1677 (A. G. I., 58-1-26); same to same, November 10, 1678 (A. G. I., 54-5-11); Salazar to the king, March 6, 1680, enclosing plans for the fort at San Marcos; Instructions by Salazar to Henrique Primo de Rivera for building a redoubt at San Marcos, December 3, 1678; Cabrera to the king, October 7, 1682 (A. G. I., 58-1-26).

border. England and Spain were nominally at peace, but this did not prevent Carolinian trade and intrigue with the Indians. Old Barbadians in Carolina proceeded as if they were still "beyond the line." The Guale missions were a menace, and their neophytes would make good slaves on Carolina plantations. Savage allies were eager to join in the work of destruction.

Early in 1680 the storm broke across the Savannah. Three hundred Indians headed by Englishmen attacked Mission Santa Catalina. Led by Captain Fuentes, commander of the guard, the inhabitants rallied to the defense. Taking refuge in the monastery, for nearly a whole day they withstood a siege. Governor Salazar despatched a relief vessel with fifty-eight men, but when they reached Santa Catalina the enemy had retired.[1]

The frightened neophytes forthwith deserted the mission. Some hurried south to

[1] For the attack on Santa Catalina, see Salazar to the king, March 6, 1680, enclosing the declarations of five runaway Englishmen (A. G. I., 58-1-26); same to same, May 14, 1680 (A. G. I., 58-1-26); printed in Serrano y Sanz, *Documentos Históricos de la Florida y la Louisiana* (Madrid, 1912), pp. 216–219. Badly translated in Brooks, *The Unwritten History of Old St. Augustine*, 137–139; Juan Marqués Cabrera to the king, December 8, 1680 (A. G. I., 54-5-11).

Zápala.   Others fled west and took refuge on
the Chattahoochee border.   With the Indians,
or close behind them, Fuentes and his soldiers
withdrew to Zápala.[1]   Governor Cabrera sent
more soldiers thither, with orders to construct
a *casa fuerte*.   It is apparently the remains of
this fort that are plainly visible on Zápala
Island to-day and are known as "The Old
Sugar House."   To hold Santa Catalina, the
King ordered families sent from the Canary
Islands; but through various mishaps they
failed to arrive.   Cabrera was instructed to
observe the treaty of 1670, which had yielded
Charleston to England; but to repel and even
pursue all intruders beyond the line.   But this
stern command did not prevent Lord Cardross
from establishing a Scotch colony at Port
Royal (1683).[2]

[1] For the retreat to Zápala, see Captain Fuentes to the
governor, Zápala, February 7, 1681; same to same, May 4, 1681;
Cabrera to the Father Provincial, May 10, 1681; Cabrera to the
king, June 14, 1681 (A. G. I., 54–5–11); The Proprietors of
Carolina to the governor and council, *Calendar of State Papers,
Colonial, America and West Indies*, March 7, 1681, No. 37; the
king of Spain to Cabrera and to the president of the Canaries,
November 10, 1681 (A. G. I., 61–6–20).   Pirate attacks are briefly
summarized in the Memorial by Echagaray, pp. 4–5 (A. G. I.,
61–6–20).

[2] For the establishment of Lord Cardross's colony, see
McCrady, *South Carolina Under the Proprietary Government*,
195–196.

The reoccupation of Santa Catalina, or even the strengthening of Zápala, was put out of question by the tightening of the hold of Carolina traders on the Guale Indians, and by savage attacks of English and French free-booters all along the coast. English trade in Indian slaves grew at an appalling rate. The Carolinians purchased captives and thus encouraged the tribes to make war on their southern neighbors. In this way the Yamassees were won over and turned against the Timucua mission Indians. The heathen Yamassees moved in a body to Santa Elena, and the disaffection spread to their Christianized relatives in the Guale missions.

Simultaneously a staggering blow was given the missions by pirate raids.[1] In 1683

[1] For the pirate raid of 1683 the manuscript materials are voluminous. See especially: Razon de lo sucedido, May 20, 1683 (A. G. I., 54–5–11); Royal cédula to governor of Florida, February 26, 1684 (A. G. I., 61–6–20); Córdova to the king, May 20, 1685 (A. G. I., 58–2–6). For plans to remove the Guale Indians southward, see Cabrera to the king, June 28, 1683; Consulta del consejo, February 10, 1684; Royal cédula to Cabrera, March 28, 1684 (A. G. I., 58–1–26); Cabrera to the king, August 26, 1684, with autos, decrees, and report of the juntas of August 21–22 (A. G. I., 54–5–11, No. 118). The raid of September-October, 1684, is set forth at length in a petition by Pérez de la Mota with accompanying proceedings in the Ranson case (A. G. I., 58–2–6). See also McCrady, *South Carolina Under the Proprietary Government*, 204–206.

the notorious "Abraham" (Agramont) plundered the missions of southern Guale, despoiled them of provisions, carried off church bells and ornaments, and killed neophytes. The survivors fled to the forests. When the scare was over the southern Guale missions were nearly ruined. Next year a Carolina vessel entered the harbor at Gualquini mission and created a new terror. During another raid by the pirate Hinckley (October, 1684) the soldiers and Indians fled from Zápala to the mainland.

Cabrera now endeavored to remove the remaining Guale missions southward to the Islands of Santa María and San Juan. But councils were divided. The missionaries, zealous and unafraid, opposed the removal. Some of the Indians sided with the padres and others with the officials.[1] In the turmoil many of the neophytes of Zápala, San Simón,

[1] For the relations of the Carolinians with the Westoes and Yamassees, see *Calendar of State Papers, Colonial, America and West Indies*, September 30, 1683, No. 1284; November 6, 1683, No. 1364; June 3, 1684, No. 1722; February 21, 1685, No. 28. See also No. 83; West to Cabrera, July 8, 1685 (A. G. I., 58–1–26, Doc. 82); Crane, "The Southern Frontier in Queen Anne's War" (*American Historical Review*, XXIV, April, 1919). For a statement of the reason for the Yamassees' flight to Carolina see Fray Joseph Ramón Escudero to Marqués de Monteleón, London, October 20, 1734 (MS.).

Tupique and Asao fled with the heathen
Yamassees to the Scotch colony at Santa
Elena. Led by Chief Altamaha, and encouraged and outfitted by Lord Cardross,
the Yamassees now made a raid clear across
Guale to the Timucua missions west of San
Agustín (February, 1685). At Santa Catalina
de Afuica early one morning they sacked the
mission, killed some of the inhabitants, and
carried off others to be sold as slaves. When
they returned, the raiders were met at the
Savannah by Lord Cardross and his men,
eager to buy their plunder.[1]

These and other disturbances helped Cabrera to carry out his plan for removing the

[1] For the Yamassee raid on Timucua, see Juan Marqués
Cabrera a Su Magestad, April 15, 1685 (A. G. I., 58–2–6, Doc.
No. 2); Autos S⁰ la entrada do los Enemigos Yngleses En las
prou.ᵃˢ de Timucua, Apalachicoli, y Caueta. Y obstilidades q.
Yntentan Hazer. Año 1685 y 1686. This contains Carta del
then.ᵗᵉ de la prou.ᵃ de timucua, March 16, 1685, and autos
giving testimony of witnesses (A. G. I., 58–1–26, Doc. No. 82)
Copia testimoniada. Los Oficiales Reales a Su Magestad,
September 30, 1686 (A. G. I., 54–5–19, Doc. No. 65); *Calendar
of State Papers, Colonial, America and West Indies*, February 21,
1685, no. 28; No. 83; Arredondo, *Demostración*, Ch. 5; Shea, *The
Catholic Church in the United States*, I, 178; Barcía, *Ensayo
Cronológico*, 287; one writer confused this Timucuan mission of
Santa Catalina with the one in northern Georgia then abandoned.
Colleton to Quiroga, undated letter (A. G. I., 58–1–26).

Guale missions. In the summer of 1686 the
pirate Agramont again appeared on the coast
and spread new terror. At the same time a
rumor was afloat that the English were
coming to destroy what was left of Guale.
Glad of protection now, most of the remaining
neophytes consented to move south to Santa
María, San Juan, and Santa Cruz islands,
which correspond to-day to Amelia Island,
Talbot Island and the coast land to the southward. Simultaneously the military head of
the province was moved from Zápala to Santa
María. With the removal of the missions the
name Guale was extended southward to
include the new district.[1]

Old Guale was ruined. But not without a
counter blow by Cabrera. He was between
pirates and Carolinians—who were not entirely distinct. With three vessels he sent
Thomás de León against Carolina (1686).
There were a hundred Spaniards in the party
and an auxiliary force of Indians. In Sep-

[1] For the withdrawal to Santa María see Swanton, J. R.,
Early History of the Creek Indians, 92, citing a royal letter of
September 9, 1688, in the Brooks MSS.; Carta de Aviso, by
Andrés Hernández to Cabrera, August 1, 1686 (A. G. I., 61–6–20.
Delgado expediente, p. 97); royal officials to crown, October 4,
1686 (A. G. I., 54–5–15. Doc. 33); Arredondo, Ch. 5; Barcía,
Ensayo Cronológico, p. 284.

tember they assaulted and completely destroyed the hated Scotch Colony at Port
Royal, which had caused so much damage.[1]
Some of the settlers they killed; others they
captured and plundered. The rest found
refuge by flight to Charleston. Among the
slain was the Indian chief from whom our old
friend Woodward had received his grant of
Santa Elena. Continuing north, at Edisto
Island, De León sacked Governor Morton's
plantation, burned seven houses, and carried
off thirteen slaves, besides other plunder
amounting to 3,000 pounds sterling. Charleston came next; but once more nature intervened to save it from the Spaniards. In a
hurricane De León's vessel, the *Rosario*, was
cast ashore, and he with others perished. A

[1] For the attack on Port Royal, see Andrés de Muñibe to the
king, Havana, February 12, 1687, transmitting declarations of
Pedro Hortelano, Joseph Juan, and others (Delgado expediente,
A. G. I., 61–6–20, p. 1). Cabrera to the king, October 6, 1687
(A. G. I., 58–1–26, no. 113). The account contained in these
documents is confirmed in all its essential details, including the
hurricane and the stranding of the vessels, in the "Introduction
to the Report on General Oglethorpe's Expedition," in Carroll,
Hist. Coll., II, 350. See also McCrady, *South Carolina under the
Proprietary Government*, 216–217; Rivers, William J., *A Sketch
of the History of South Carolina to the Close of the Proprietary
Government by the Revolution of 1719* (Charleston, 1856), 143, 144;
Appendix, 425–443; Carroll, *Hist. Collections*, I, 83.

second vessel was beached by the storm and then burned. In it perished a captive brother-in-law of the governor. With the third vessel the expedition limped back to San Agustín. Cabrera was even with Lord Cardross.

The destruction of Port Royal came in the midst of squabbling at Charleston. Half angry, half frightened, the colonists rose up in arms. They appealed to the Proprietors; they complained of "unpreparedness." In a Parliament it was decided to strike a counter blow. Two French buccaneering vessels were fitted out and manned with two hundred good pirates and three hundred Carolinians. But the expedition did not sail.[1] England and Spain were nominally at peace, and the new governor, James Colleton, promised a noosed rope for anyone who might persist in the

[1] For the failure of plans for a counter blow, see Governor Richard Cony to the Earl of Sunderland, December 2, 1686, *Calendar of State Papers, Colonial, America and West Indies*, No. 1029. The Proprietors to Colleton, March 3, 1687, *ibid.*, No. 1161; same to same, October 10, 1687, *ibid.*, No. 1457; McCrady, *South Carolina under the Proprietary Government*, 218–229. Rivers, *A Sketch of the History of South Carolina*, Appendix, 425, 443, 444. Barcía, *Ensayo Cronológico*, 286; Carroll, *Hist. Coll.*, II, 350. For the activities of some of the buccaneers between 1680 and 1690 see Jameson, J. F., *Privateering and Piracy in the Colonial Period: Illustrative Documents* (N. Y., 1923), 84–147.

enterprise. The Proprietors in England approved Colleton's stand. The Carolinians themselves were to blame, they said. Charleston had harbored pirates; the Scots had abetted the Yamassees. The Carolinians could only smother their wrath and await a better day.

CHAPTER IV

THE CONTEST FOR WESTERN GEORGIA
(1680–1725)

The Spaniards had been driven from old Guale. Meantime a similar contest in the hinterland had begun. From Charleston the English traders led the onslaught. From Apalache (Tallahassee) the Spanish missionaries and soldiers went forth to stem the tide.

To the westward the Georgia tribes beckoned the Englishmen across the Savannah to a life of adventure and freedom, and to profitable trade in skins and slaves. The trails through their villages led to fabled mines of silver and gold, and to the shores of the great Spanish Lake (the Gulf of Mexico), on which more than one English buccaneer had already sailed. Relentlessly the Carolinians advanced. In vain the Spaniards tried to hold them back. The game was played by diplomacy, trade, and war. The chief pawn in the sport was the Red Man between.

Each year the Carolinians visited tribes more and more remote. Charleston was not a year old when Dr. Henry Woodward visited Cufitachiqui. Four years later he crossed the Savannah to the Westoes.[1]

The Spaniards were on the *qui vive*. In the very year when Woodward crossed the middle Savannah (1674) the Apalachicolas (Lower Creeks, the English called them) opportunely asked for missionaries. There may have been some connection between the two events. These tribes lived on the middle Chattahoochee below the falls. They had made more than one such petition in vain, but now their voice was heard. The English danger served as a magna vox. So to the Apalachicola Confederacy Fray Juan Ocón and two newcomers were sent in 1679 to set

[1] For the early explorations of the Virginians in the West, see Alvord and Bidgood, *The First Explorations of the Trans-Alleghany Region by the Virginians, 1650–1674* (Cleveland, 1912). For Woodward's journey to Cufitachiqui in 1670, see *Shaftesbury Papers*, 183, 201, 265, 216–217; for his expedition to Virginia in 1671, see *ibid.*, 210, 220, 300–307, 337–338, 345, 349; his visit to the Westoes in 1674 is treated *ibid.*, 441, 443, 445, 446, 456–462. See also *Calendar of State Papers, Colonial, America and West Indies*, April 10, 1677, nos. 176, 177, 180; McCrady, *South Carolina under the Proprietary Government*, 177. For early Carolina Indian trade, see Crane, V. W., *American Historical Review*, XXIV, 379–380.

up the Cross at Sábacola, a village on the Chattahoochee a few leagues below the falls. Their hopes were destined to a shock. The Gran Cacique, or Emperor, of the Cavetas (Cowetas), head tribe of the Confederacy, had not been consulted. Three days after the friars arrived this potentate descended the river and ordered them out. Heavy-hearted, Father Ocón and his companions withdrew to Apalache.

Hard-fisted Cabrera now became governor. The trouble, he concluded, was that the friars had gone to Sábacola without soldiers. So in March, 1681, two wide-brimmed Franciscans, accompanied by seven uniformed infantrymen, rowed up the Chattahoochee once more to Sábacola. In May Father Gutiérrez wrote glowing accounts of success.[1] He had hopes of baptizing even the Gran Cacique himself. But his dream soon faded.

[1] For early relations with the Apalachicolas and the founding of the Sábacola mission, see Castro to the King of Spain, August 22, 1639; Aranguíz to the King of Spain, September 8, 1662 (A. G. I., 54–5–10); Hita Salazar to the king, November 23, 1675; Hita Salazar to the king, March 8, 1680; Cabrera to the king, December 8, 1680; Carta de Fray Pedro Gutiérrez, May 19, 1681; Cabrera to the king, two letters, June 14, 1681; Carta de Fray Miguel Abengojar, July 3, 1681 (A. G. I., 54–5–11); same to same, October 7, 1682 (*ibid.*, Doc. no. 95).

Within a few months the Indians became hostile, and soldiers and friars withdrew. English influence was suspected by the Spaniards. Cabrera threatened and a compromise resulted. The Christianized portion of the Sábacolas moved down the river to the junction of the Chattahoochee and the Pedernales (Flint). There they were established in the mission of Santa Cruz de Sábacola, near the recently formed mission of the Chatots.

The English tide rolled on. Carolinians fell out with the Westoes and by 1682 the tribe had been practically exterminated.[1] The way was open now for the English traders to the Apalachicolas. Woodward again led the van. With half a dozen hardy followers, in the summer of 1685 he was on the Chattahoochee, where he introduced himself to the Gran Cacique at Caveta. His presence there brought on another border clash with the Spaniards. The documents incident to it

[1] For troubles of the Carolinians with the Westoes, see *Calendar of State Papers, Colonial, America and West Indies*, May 17, 1680, No. 1357; February 21, 1681, Nos. 26 and 27; March 7, 1681, No. 37; March 9, 1681, No. 39. For Woodward's commission, see *ibid.*, May 10, 1682, No. 499; for his pardon, *ibid.*, May 23, 1682, No. 518. See also Crane, V. W., *American Anthropologist*, N. S. XX, 331; Swanton, *Early History of the Creek Indians*, 307.

Plan of the Apalachicola Fort, 1689. From the original in the
Spanish Archives.

bring the Apalachicolas at that period out of hazy conjecture into the clear light of history. The Anglo-Spanish contest for western Georgia thus begun lasted till 1763.

News of Woodward's doings caused a stir at Apalache. Antonio Matheos, commander there, now assumed the character of defender of the Chattahoochee border. Governor Cabrera sent soldiers to reinforce the Apalache garrison. Without awaiting them Matheos hurried west and north with a force of Spaniards and two hundred and fifty mission Indians. His primary aim was to capture Woodward and his men and to punish the vassals of Spain who had admitted these foreigners. On his way up the Chattahoochee to the falls, where Columbus now stands, he passed through eight or more of the villages which later were known to the English as the Lower Creeks. Their location was very much the same as that which they occupied a century later.

Indians and Englishmen fled. Of all the chiefs Old Pentocolo, of the village of Apalachicola, alone dared risk his neck. Before he went in hiding Woodward penned a defiant note to Matheos declaring that next time he would be strong enough to stand his ground. "I am very sorry that I came with so small a following that I cannot await your arrival. Be informed that I came to get acquainted with the country, its mountains, the seacoast, and Apalache. I trust in God that I shall meet you gentlemen later when I have a larger following. September 2, 1685. *Vale.*" Near the falls Matheos destroyed a half-finished stockade built by the Indians under the direction of the Englishmen. Leaving spies in the country, he then returned to San Luís, after nearly a month's futile chase.[1]

Woodward no doubt smiled as Matheos withdrew. Scarcely had the Spaniards turned their backs when the Englishmen emerged from their hiding places and began to operate once more in the Apalachicola towns. The news was carried to Matheos by the spies. So back he posted late in December with a larger force than before. Cabrera's wrath was now stirred, and he ordered Matheos, in case the Indians refused to deliver the Englishmen, to burn their towns.

[1] The first expedition of Matheos is set forth in Woodward's defiant note to Matheos, September 2, 1685 (A. G. I., 58–4–23); Matheos to Governor Cabrera, Casista, September 21, 1685; Domingo de Leturiondo to Cabrera, San Luís, November 5, 1685 (A. G. I., 58–1–26, Doc. 82).

This time Matheos went overland to Sábacola el Grande. Crossing the Chattahoochee there, he went by roundabout trails in an endeavor to make a surprise attack on the Englishmen. Near Caveta he confiscated from a blockhouse five hundred deerskins and other merchandise belonging to the invaders. But his efforts to capture Woodward and his men were in vain. Once more they and the natives had taken to the woods.

Aided by Chief Pentocolo Matheos now summoned the absconding headmen to Caveta. Eight villages reluctantly responded, but the chiefs of the four northern towns stubbornly refused to appear. The eight towns which submitted were pardoned. The others—Caveta, Casista, Tasquique, and Colone—were burned to ashes. While the embers were still smoking Matheos returned homeward. Thirty disabled men he sent down the Chattahoochee in canoes. With the rest he went to San Luís by land.[1]

[1] For Matheos's second expedition to Caveta, see Matheos to Cabrera, Caveta, January 12, 1686; San Luís, February 8, 1686; San Luís, March 14, 1686; Cabrera to the viceroy, March 19, 1686 (A. G. I., 58–4–23); Cabrera to the viceroy, March 19, 1686 (A. G. I., 58–1–26, Doc. 102).

The destroyed towns repented, and five weeks after Matheos returned Pentocolo was sent to ask mercy for them. But Matheos suspected crocodile tears. His suspicions were well founded, for as soon as the Spaniards left Caveta the Englishmen once more emerged from their hiding places and continued to trade. Some of them soon returned to Charleston, leaving Woodward ill at Casista. Late in summer he too departed, carried on a stretcher by the Indians, and followed by one hundred and fifty Apalachicola braves laden with peltry.[1] On their way home four of his men were killed and plundered by Guale Indians, allies of the Spaniards. The English traders to Apalachicola were not yet safe from a flank attack.

Woodward never returned to the Apalachicolas, it seems, but he had shown the way,

[1] For the repentance of the Apalachicolas, the return of the English to the Apalachicolas, and of Woodward and his men to Charleston, see Cabrera to the king, March 22, 1686; same to same, May 29, 1686 (A. G. I., 58–1–26, docs. 104, 106); Matheos to Cabrera, San Luís, May 19, 1686; same to same, May 21, 1686; Cabrera to viceroy, June 2, 1686; the viceroy to the king, July 19, 1686; junta de guerra, Mexico, July 20, 1686 (all in A. G. I., 58–4–23); Cabrera to the viceroy, July 22, 1686; Matheos to Cabrera, August 21, 1686 (both in A. G. I., 61–6–20); Cabrera to the king, November 8, 1686, with enclosures (A. G. I., 54–5–12, doc. 39).

and next season other Carolinians went to
the Chattahoochee. Cabrera sent a third
expedition to capture them. When Quiroga
became governor (1687) the Apalachicolas
complained bitterly of the burning of their
towns. Quiroga consoled them and they
renewed their allegiance. But this did not
keep the English out. They kept coming each
season and Quiroga in turn was forced to send
two expeditions to capture them. Five such
campaigns had thus been made against these
Carolina traders in less than five years. But
they were all in vain. The Anglomen were
fully protected by the natives, for they had
good merchandise at low prices.

There was only one thing to be done, said
Quiroga. A garrison must be established on
the Chattahoochee. To build the fort, late
in 1689 he sent Captain Primo de Rivera.
It was placed at the village of Apalachicola,
south of Caveta. At the end of two months
it was completed, with stockade, parapet,
ditch and four bastions. To guard it Fabián
de Angulo was left with twenty soldiers and
twenty Apalache Indians. In an assembly
at Caveta, in the following May, the chiefs
promised Angulo to join hands with the

Spaniards to keep the English out. They now had "but one word and one heart," both Spanish.[1]

The Spanish policy seemed for a moment to have succeeded. In reality it had miscarried. The burning of the towns and the establishment of the fort in their midst were designed to keep the Indians loyal and the English out. Neither result followed. Instead the Indians were alienated. Most of them now abandoned their homes on the Chattahoochee and moved eastward to join the Uchis on the Ocmulgee. Thither the English promptly followed them. The Ocmulgee now became known to the English as Ocheese (Uchis) Creek, and the Indians as the Creeks. In Spanish circles, in a similar way, the Apalachicolas gradually became known as Uchis.

[1] For Spanish relations with the Apalachicolas during 1687–1690 and the building of the fort, see Quiroga to the king, April 1, 1688 (A. G. I., 54–5–12, doc. 61, published in Serrano y Sanz, *Documentos Históricos de la Florida y la Luisiana*, 219–221); Quiroga to the king, April 15, 1688; same to same, September 29, 1689; same to same, June 8, 1690, with accompanying documents relative to the building of the fort (with drawing), on the Chattahoochee (A. G. I., 54–5–12); same to same, August 21, 1690 (A. G. I., 54–5–13, Doc. 13, A.B.C.).

It is the records of a dispute which reveal this new information concerning the migration of the Creeks.[1] Quiroga asked the provincial for missionaries for the new outpost on the Chattahoochee. An argument ensued. Father Luna maintained that the Indians, afraid of the garrison, had fled east, "to find favor with the English." Quiroga denied the charge. He was able to prove that some of the Apalachicolas were still on the Chattahoochee; but it is equally clear by his own admission that some of them had moved east

[1] Both Swanton and Crane were unable to determine the location of the Lower Creeks before 1690. Both have left the question a matter of speculation. Swanton writes: "South Carolina documents place this tribe [the Kasihta] on Ocheese Creek in 1702, Ocheese Creek being an old name for the upper part of the Ocmulgee, and it seems probable from an examination of the Spanish documents that they were settled there as early as 1680–1685." Commenting on Matheos's report of May 19, 1686, Swanton infers that the four towns burned by Matheos were probably on the Ocmulgee. Of course his conclusion is incorrect (Swanton, J. R., *Early History of the Creek Indians*, 220–221 (Washington, 1922). In another connection Swanton says that in 1681 the Coweta were living in the neighborhood of Butts County, Georgia. *Ibid.*, 307; Crane, V. W. ("The Southern Frontier During Queen Anne's War," *Am. Hist. Rev.*, XXIV, 381), implies that the Kawita and Kasihta (which he makes synonymous with Oconee and Ocheese) were on the Oconee in 1684. For the naming of the Lower Creeks see Crane, *Mississippi Valley Historical Review*, V, 339. For the identity of the Westo, see Crane, *American Anthropologist*, N. S., XX, 331.

to the Uchis. Thus is solved the mystery of the appearance of the Lower Creeks on the Ocmulgee.

The Apalachicola presidio was short-lived. In the summer of 1691 corsairs again threatened San Agustín. Soldiers were sorely needed and the garrison was withdrawn. In order that the English on the "Rio de Uchise" might not occupy it, the fort was destroyed and even the ditches filled in.[1]

The defection of the Apalachicolas from Spanish allegiance did not end with the desertion of their home lands. It turned into active war on the missions of Apalache and Timucua, and on the Indians there who had taken part in the burning of their towns. Englishmen lived among the Apalachicolas, stirred them up, and even led them in their assaults. Torres, the new governor, launched another campaign (1694), in which fifty captives were taken.[2] A lively dispute now

[1] For the call for missionaries, the abandonment of the fort, and the eastward migration of the Apalachicolas, see Quiroga to the king, April 10, 1692 (A. G. I., 54–5–13, Doc. No. 32); same to same, April 18, 1792 (*ibid.*, Doc. 36); same to same April 30, 1692 (*ibid.*, Doc. 42).

[2] Swanton (p. 221), citing Serrano y Sanz, gives the date of Torres's expedition as 1695, but the documents show that it was in 1694.

followed over boundaries. Governors Smith
and Blake claimed the Apalachicola country
for Carolina. Torres branded the claims as
preposterous. Archdale was conciliatory, but
he warned the Spaniards to keep out of
Apalachicola.[1]

While Spaniards fought and protested, the
Carolina Indian trade grew apace. Englishmen soon passed beyond the Chattahoochee
to the Alabamas and Chickasaws.[2] The
rapidity of their advance was an index of the
growing demand for Indian slaves. The
climax of greed was reached while Moore was

[1] For Apalachicola relations and boundary disputes, 1694–
1700, see Torres to Governor Smith, August 5, 1694 (A. G. I.,
58–1–26, No. 132). Torres to the king, March 11, 1695 (A. G.
I., 58–1–26, Doc. 130, in Serrano y Sanz, *Documentos Históricos*,
224–227); Torres to the king, July 8, 1695, with related documents concerning boundaries (A. G. I., 58–1–26, No. 132);
Torres to Governor Archdale, January 24, 1695 (Archdale
Papers, Library of Congress); Archdale to the Governor of
Florida, January 24, 1696; same to same, April 4, 1696 (Archdale
Papers, Library of Congress); Torres to the king, February 7,
1697 (A. G. I., 58–1–26, Doc. 131).

[2] For the Carolina Indian trade in the last decade of the
century, see Crane, *American Historical Review*, XXIV, 379–
382. See also Carroll, *Hist. Coll.*, II, 88–89, 107–108, 118–121;
Journal of the Council of South Carolina, December 12, 1699;
E. Randolph to the Lords of Trade, in Rivers, *A Sketch of the
History of South Carolina*, 443. A Carolina view of Moore's
trading activities is given in a "Representation and Address,"
printed in Rivers, *ibid.*, 455–456.

governor (1700–1702). A new impetus was given to the traffic by the settlement of the French at Biloxi. Excitable Carolinians feared a French attack on Charleston. Some of them talked of fleeing to England; but the more manly favored a counter blow and a more aggressive trade policy.

The Carolinians now found two rivals blocking the way to the Alabamas. The first obstacles to be removed were the Spaniards and Indians of Apalache. On them the Apala-chicola-English raids continued. In May, 1702, the Timucua mission of Santa Fé was destroyed. To retaliate, Governor Zuñiga sent Captain Uriza with a force of Spaniards and eight hundred Indians against the Apalachi-colas and their English abettors. At that very moment Englishmen, headed by a "Captain Antonio," were holding war councils in Caveta. A double blow was to be struck at the Spaniards. While a fleet captured San Agustín, traders and the Apalachicolas were to destroy Apalache. In preparation for the fray a fort was built at Caveta. On the same day that Uriza left Bacuqua, Captain Antonio led several hundred braves forth from Achito. They met near the Pedernales (Flint). By a trick the Spanish force was defeated. The battle ground was strewn with dead and dying Apalaches; others were captured; the rest fled in dismay, leaving baggage behind. The Spanish soldiery showed nearly equal speed. All Florida was now terrorized. The Apalache settlements were ordered consolidated close to San Luís; San Agustín was put under arms; and Governor Zuñiga sent calls for help to Spain and Mexico.[1]

Zuñiga's fears were justified, for Queen Anne's War was now proclaimed in America. Governor Moore in person led the expedition planned against San Agustín. As he went down the coast he spread devastation. The

[1] For Uriza's campaign, see Iberville to Francisco Martínez, January 3, 1702, Margry, *Découvertes et Etablissements des Français dans l'Amerique Septentrionale* (Paris, 1875–1886), IV, 579; Shea, J. G., *The Catholic Church in the United States*, I, 459; Zuñiga to the king, September 30, 1702 (A. G. I., 58–1–27, Doc. 58); Manuel Solano to the king, October 22, 1702 (Demanda Puesta, A. G. I., 58–2–18); Francisco Romo de Uriza to Zuñiga, October 22, 1702 (*ibid.*); autos and report regarding defence at San Agustín, October 27, and November 1 (*ibid.*). The campaign was approved in Royal Council, August 23, 1703, nearly a year after Uriza's defeat (*ibid.*); Mitchell's Map of 1755 (Swanton, *Early History of the Creek Indians*, plates 3 and 6). See also Crane, *Am. Hist. Rev.*, XXIV, 385; McCrady, *South Carolina under the Proprietary Government*, 379–380; Rivers, *A Sketch of the History of South Carolina*, 199–200; Carroll, *Hist. Coll.*, II, 351; Swanton, *Early History of the Creek Indians*, 120–121.

three transplanted Guale missions were committed to the flames and three friars were captured. Thus it was that the Spanish frontier fell back another step, from the Santa María to the San Juan. The Carolinians took the city of San Agustín, but after a siege lasting nearly a month they failed to capture the sturdy stone fortress outside the gates.[1]

Moore, no longer governor, was given a chance to retrieve his lost reputation by a new campaign against Apalache—that Apalache which stood in the road to Pensacola and Mobile. In December, 1703, he set forth from Charleston. When he left the Ocmulgee he had in his train fifty Englishmen and a thousand Indian allies. The Apalache missions had served the red men three-quarters of a century; now they were doomed. The first blow was struck at the fortified town of Ayubale. Father Miranda directed the defence. The fight lasted nearly all day, and

[1] For Moore's expedition against San Agustín, see Rivers, *A Sketch of the History of South Carolina* (Charleston, 1856), pp. 197–204, 453–456; Crane, *Am. Hist. Rev.*, vol. XXIV, p. 386; McCrady, *South Carolina, 1670–1719*, 378, 391; Carroll, *Hist. Coll.*, II, 351–352; Shea, J. G., *Catholic Church in the United States*, 459–460; Fairbanks, *History of Florida* (Philadelphia, 1871), 174; Barcía, *Ensayo Cronológico*, 320.

the Spaniards yielded only when their am-
munition gave out. Several Englishmen fell;
twenty-five defenders were slain and over one
hundred and fifty captured. Of his exploit
Moore wrote, "I never see or hear of a stouter
or braver thing done." Near Ayubale Moore
defeated Lieutenant Mexía and the garrison
of San Luís. A number of prisoners taken
were tortured; Father Parga was burned at
the stake and beheaded while Mexía looked
on from the stocks. Shortly afterward Mexía
himself, Father Miranda, and four soldiers
met a like fate. One town bought immunity
with the church ornaments and ten horses
loaded with provisions. Of fourteen missions
this was the only one not destroyed.[1] When
Moore withdrew eastward he took with him

[1] For Moore's campaign against Apalache, see Crane, *Am.
Hist. Rev.*, XXIV, 386–387; Moore, "An account of what the
army did under command of Col. Moore, in his expedition last
winter, against the Spaniards and Spanish Indians. In a letter
from the said Col. Moore to the governor of Carolina. Printed
in the *Boston News*, May 1, 1704." (Carroll, *Historical Collections of South Carolina*, II, 574–576; Zuñiga to the king, March
30, 1704 (Swanton, J. R., *Early History of the Creek Indians*,
122–123); letter of Bienville to his home government (printed
in Swanton, *ibid.*, 123); "Statements made in the Introduction
to the Report on General Oglethorpe's Expedition to St. Augustine" (Carroll, *Hist. Coll.*, II, 352–353); Shea, *History of the
Catholic Church in the United States*, I, 461–462; Rivers, *Sketch*,
207–209.

1400 mission Indians. Part of them were enslaved; the rest were established on the Savannah River, safely between Charleston and the Apalachicola allies. Moore wrote to Governor Johnson, "We have made Carolina as safe as the conquest of Apalatchia can make it."

Moore's savage attack was a mortal blow to the Apalache missions. Later the fragments were reassembled round a new presidio at San Marcos, on the Gulf coast. To the end of Queen Anne's War the English were free to live and trade among the Apalachicolas (Lower Creeks), whose towns—eleven in number in 1709—were now ranged along the Ocmulgee River.

Apalache annihilated, it was the aim of the Carolinians next to destroy Pensacola, uproot the French of Mobile, and extend trade and dominion to the Father of Waters. In this great game the western Georgia Indians still participated; but the struggle now turned on the control of the Alabama Creeks, next beyond, and of the Chickasaws and Choctaws further west. English and French traders alike donned the war paint and conducted their partisans to battle. The English won over the Alabamas, led them against Pensacola, and against the Choctaws who protected Mobile. But the able Frenchman, Bienville, won back the Alabamas. Peace in 1714 left Pensacola and Mobile intact, and the French secure in the Alabama basin.[1]

Suddenly an event occurred which sent the Apalachicolas back to the Chattahoochee to live, and restored Spanish influence among them. It was a case of poetic justice. The Yamassees had been Carolina's chief instruments in the destruction of Spanish Guale. They now headed a widespread revolt against the English and returned to Spanish allegiance. The first blow fell in May, 1715, at the Yamassee town of Pocotaligo. By the middle of June the revolt east of the Savannah had been snuffed out, but not before two hundred Carolinians had been slain. The Yamassees

[1] For the Alabama country during Queen Anne's War, see Crane, "The Southern Frontier in Queen Anne's War" (*American Historical Review*, vol. XXIV, 379–395; Margry, *Découvertes et Etablissements des Français*, IV; Rivers, *Sketch*, pp. 231–237, gives a report on western trade in 1708. The same is given in *Calendar of State Papers, Colonial, America and West Indies*, 1708–9, p. 468. For attacks on Pensacola in 1712, see Salinas Varona to the viceroy, January 16, and July 16, 1713 (A. G. I., 61–1–34, pp. 31–32. See also document *ibid.*, pp. 89–90); Barcía, *Ensayo Cronológico*, 328.

now fled to San Agustín where they were welcomed by the ringing of church bells.[1]

The disaffection spread west to the Creeks and other tribes. Here was Spain's chance and quickly she seized it. When the uprising occurred, Old Brimins, the Emperor of Caveta, called a council of the Lower Creek chiefs. They decided to make peace with the Spaniards. Englishmen among them were evicted, imprisoned, or slain. An embassy was sent to Pensacola.[2] There on July 7, forty Creek chiefs and headmen delivered Spanish captives, and enacted peace ceremonies. Seven chiefs of the Western (Upper) Creeks went to Mexico and swore allegiance to the King in the presence of the viceroy. They were lavishly entertained and they marvelled at

[1] The Yamassee-Creek war is treated by Crane, *Am. Hist. Rev.*, XXIV, 394; McCrady, *South Carolina under the Proprietary Government*, 1670–1719, 513–543; Swanton, J. R., *Early History of the Creek Indians*, 97–102, 225–226. Osgood, Herbert L., *The American Colonies in the Eighteenth Century*, II, 347–352. (New York, 1924). Contemporary narratives are "An account of Missionaries sent to South Carolina" (in Carroll, *Hist. Coll.*, II, 527–568); "Account of the Breaking Out of the Yamassee War," *Boston News*, June 13, 1715 (Carroll, *Hist. Coll.*, II, 569–572). Escudero to Marqués de Monteleón, Spanish ambassador at London, Madrid, February 17, 1716.

[2] An anonymous French account of the uprising at Caveta is given in Swanton, *op. cit.*, 225–226. The episode is made the theme of a novel in *The Yamassee*, by William Gilmore Simms.

St. Simons (Gualquini) Sound, looking seaward.

the wonders of the metropolis of North America.[1] Meanwhile the Lower Creeks gave obedience at San Agustín and made intermittent war on Carolina.

For a decade now Spanish and English diplomats waged a battle for supremacy among the Creeks. At Caveta two factions formed in the Indian councils. Old Brimins, the Emperor, leaned toward the English; his son, the usingulo Chipacasi (Seepey Coffee), was a staunch supporter of the Spaniards. Numerous contests occurred between the Spanish and English agents who met at the Indian towns in the struggle for control. One such took place in 1717. Diego de Peña, head of an embassy from San Agustín, encountered a party of English traders at Caveta.[2] The chiefs held a heated debate.

---

[1] For the Creek visits to Pensacola and Mexico, see Salinas Varona to Governor Ayala, Pensacola, July 24, 1717 (Serrano y Sanz, *Documentos Históricos*, 238–240); same to same, September 9, 1717 (*ibid.*, 240–242).

[2] For the visit to San Agustín in 1717 of the Usingulo and war chief Chislacaliche, see letter of Governor Ayala quoted in Swanton, *Early History of the Creek Indians*, 125. For Peña's embassy to Caveta, see "Diario del Viaje que hizo el Teniente Diego Peña á Apalachicola," beginning at Sávacola on September 20, 1717 (Serrano y Sanz, *Documentos Históricos*, 227–237; Barcía, *Ensayo Cronológico*, 329, 356–357, 361.

The Emperor adhered to the English, his son to the Spaniards. Chipacasi's oratory and Peña's whiskey were plied in vain, and Peña was forced to leave under escort to prevent a massacre. But it was a drawn battle, for at the same time ten of the English party were expelled from Talapoosa, an Upper Creek town.

This tilt is typical of the decade. A few months after Peña withdrew from Caveta Juan Fernández and a party of soldiers escorted to their homes the Talapoosa chiefs who had been to Mexico City. At Teguale Emperor Brimins, Chipacasi, and a delegation of Lower Creek chiefs, in formal ceremony ratified what had been done in Mexico. The celebrations were interrupted by a messenger who told of the arrival of John Musgrove and thirty Englishmen at Caveta. Brimins, Fernández and Chipacasi hurried east and another factional struggle ensued. In the end the English were expelled and the Fernández party withdrew. It was another drawn battle.[1]

[1] The diplomatic mission of Juan Fernández to the Creeks in 1718 is set forth at length in Barcía, *Ensayo Cronológico*, pp. 331–340.

Spanish influence was now strengthened by a new presidio at San Marcos (1718). Scattered Apalaches were reassembled, and new missions were established there. Some of the Creeks, too, moved south to live close at hand.[1] But in time good bargains told in favor of the English. Though it was no one-sided matter, in 1725 Tobias Fitch made real progress. On an official visit for Carolina he went several times back and forth among the Upper and Lower Creeks. He organized a campaign against the hated Yamassees, who now lived under the shelter of San Agustín. The Upper Creeks were friendly and readily joined the war party, but the Lower Creeks were "unserton." At Caveta Fitch encountered and struggled with a Spanish embassy from San Marcos. Old Brimins was still friendly to the English. Chipacasi had been loyal to Spain ever since the Yamassee uprising. But now, by the aid of the Emperor, Fitch won him over and he joined the campaign against the Yamassees. It was a signal

[1] For the presidio and the new missions at San Marcos, see Barcía, *Ensayo Cronológico*, 343–346, 348; Fray Joseph Ramón Escudero to Marqués de Monteleón, London, October 20, 1734 (MS.); extract of the same quoted in Swanton, *Early History of the Creek Indians*, 102.

victory.[1]   Nevertheless, the down river towns
—Seminoles they became—still clung to
Spain. With the rest the English were for the
time in the ascendant, but for the next
thirty-five years constant vigilance was the
price of success.

[1] The mission of Tobias Fitch to the Creeks is recounted in
Mereness, Newton D., *Travels in the American Colonies* (New
York, 1916), pp. 175–212.

CHAPTER V

DIPLOMATIC CONTROVERSIES OVER FORT KING GEORGE AND OGLETHORPE'S COLONY

(1721–1738)

The Yamassee-Creek war shocked the Carolina colony into a sense of its insecurity, and there followed a movement for the defense of the southern border. Inevitably this southward advance of the English brought on new struggles with the Spaniards.

Sir Robert Montgomery's fantastic scheme for Azilia (1718) never got beyond the paper stage, but it was symbolic of the desire for a buffer colony. Soon after Azilia went up in rhetoric, Colonel John Barnwell was sent to build Fort King George at the mouth of the Altamaha (1721). It was planted close to the site of one of the old Spanish missions.

Now it was the Spaniard's turn to sound the alarm. Governor Benavides protested to Governor Nicholson. On the other side of the Atlantic a diplomatic joust was held by Newcastle and Pozobueno. England stood on the Carolina grant of 1665, which extended to 29°. Spain's reply was obvious. England could not grant what she did not possess. Charles II's paper grant had included a line of Spanish settlements all the way from Santa Catalina to San Agustín, a stretch of one hundred and fifty miles.[1] In 1670, when the two nations adopted the principle of actual possession, England did not hold a foot of soil south of Charleston. The debate waxed warm. Then Spain proposed that the governors of Carolina and Florida be commissioned to fix the boundary in accord with the treaty of 1670. England agreed, and Spain appointed commissioners. In March, 1725, Menéndez Marqués and Joseph Primo de Rivera arrived at Charleston. Dressed in their best they presented their instructions.

[1] For Azilia, see Jones, C. C., *History of Georgia* (Boston, 1883), I, 70–75; *South Carolina Historical Society Collections* (Charleston, 1858), II, 232–233. For Fort King George on the Altamaha, see *ibid.*, Vol. I, 232, 235, 236, 237, 239, 243, 281, 285, 295, 296; Vol. II, 144, 148, 154, 155, 169, 170, 171, 179; Smith, W. R., *South Carolina as a Royal Province* (New York, 1903), 208–209; McCrady, *South Carolina under the Proprietary Government, 1670–1719*, 575, 577; Carroll, B. R., *Historical Collections of South Carolina*, I, 236, 240, 254, 257–259, 269, 278, 280, 281, 282–292. Jones, *History of Georgia*, (I, 68), erroneously locates Fort King George at the junction of the Oconee and Ocmulgee. For Benavides's plan to capture Charleston in 1719, see Barcía, *Ensayo Cronológico*, 341–343, 350–354; McCrady, *History of South Carolina Under Royal Government, 1719–1776*, 32, 35, 53–54, (New York, 1899).

Surprised enough they were to be told by President Middleton that he had no orders in the matter. For two more years the English flag waved over the Altamaha; then Fort King George was abandoned, but not because of the Spanish protest.[1]

The need of a buffer colony continued and Georgia was founded. The charter assigned to the Trustees the region between the Savannah and the Altamaha, and westward to the Pacific. What cared King George that the grant cut a wide swath through Florida, Louisiana, and Texas? Or that, incidentally, it included Albuquerque, Socorro, and other New Mexico settlements? Oglethorpe ar-

[1] Records of the negotiations between Newcastle and Pozobueno, and between Governor Benavides and the officials at Charleston (1724–1725) are given in "Testimonio de los autos y demas diligencias fechas sobre la division de los terminos de esta jurisdicción, y la de Carolina, en virtud de las dos reales zédulas que en ellos se contienen, sus fechas 10 de junio y 18 de Agosto de 1724 (A. G. I., 58–1–31. Printed in Serrano y Sanz, *Documentos Históricos de la Florida y la Luisiana*, pp. 243–260.) See also Arredondo, *Demostración*, ch. 6; Smith, *South Carolina*, 208–209; Carroll, *Historical Collections*, I, 269–271; McCrady, *History of South Carolina, 1719–1776*, 74–78; *South Carolina Historical Society Collections*, Vol. I (1857), pp. 234–239; Jones, *History of Georgia*, I, 68–69; Stevens, *History of Georgia*, I, 145; Benavides to the king, April 21, 1722, concerning Fort King George and the mission of Menéndez to protest, enclosing letter to the Governor of South Carolina, February 11, 1722 (Brooks, *op. cit.*, 168–170).

rived in 1733 and Savannah quickly arose on the site of Musgrove's trading post. Darien on the Altamaha and Frederica on St. Simons soon followed. The Altamaha was the southern limit of the Georgia grant, but Oglethorpe did not stop here. He was standard bearer for England, not alone for Georgia, and he had military ambitions. So down the coast he pushed his fortifications to the very shadow of San Agustín.[1]

A new diplomatic battle now took place. Geraldino protested in the name of Spain;[2]

[1] For the founding of Georgia, see McCrady, *History of South Carolina under the Royal Government, 1719–1776*, 113–115; Jones, *History of Georgia*, I, chs. 4–12; Stevens, *History of Georgia*, I, 57–140; M'Call, Hugh, *History of Georgia* (1811, 1816; reprinted, Atlanta, 1909. The reprint is here cited); *Colonial Records of Georgia* (Atlanta, 1904 to date, cited *Ga. Col. Rec.*), vol. I. For official opinion in England on pushing the forts beyond the Altamaha, see *Diary of the First Earl of Egmont (Viscount Percival), Historical Manuscripts Commission*, vol. II, 1734–1738 (London, 1923), 141, 159, 181, 183, 285–286; *South Carolina Historical Society Collections*, II, 264. For Oglethorpe's return to England in 1734, see Egmont's *Diary*, II, 112. For Tomochichi at the Court of London, *ibid.*, 113–118, 121–126. For Oglethorpe's demand for soldiers (1735), see Egmont's *Diary*, II, 141, 159, 166, 183, 187, 201–204.

[2] For the Spanish protest against the founding of Georgia, see Arredondo, *Demostración*, ch. 6. Fray Joseph Ramón Escudero's communication to Marqués de Monteleón, Spanish ambassador in London, October 20, 1734, was written while Tomochici was there. He suggests a combination of French, Spaniards, and Indians to expel the English (MS., Library of Congress).

Newcastle replied for England. The old
arguments were thrashed over, and Charles
Dempsey was sent to America to assist in the
negotiations. Like a shuttle-cock he darted
back and forth between Georgia and Florida.
Oglethorpe insisted on the San Juan River as
a boundary, and backed his demand with
soldiers.[1] Then Güemes y Horcasitas sent
Antonio de Arredondo from Havana to Frederica to demand English retreat beyond Port
Royal. Florida and Georgia were on the
verge of war. At last, after many parleys,
Oglethorpe and Governor Sánchez signed a
treaty.[2] All boundary questions were left for

[1] This demand was made plausible, to the innocent government at home, by a map showing a southern mouth of the
Altamaha debouching near the St. Marys.

[2] For the Dempsey and Arredondo negotiations and the
Sánchez treaty, see Jones, *History of Georgia*, I, 239–252; Stevens,
History of Georgia, I, 145–149; Wright, Robert, *A Memoir of
General James Oglethorpe* (London, 1867), chs. 8–9; *Georgia
Colonial Records*, XXI, 77, 86, 104, 115, 122, 123, 144, 150, 154,
155, 160–161, 206–207, 212, 218, 224–226, 236, 271, 284, 362–
363 (this contains a summary), 376; XXII, Pt. I, 219; Egmont's
Diary, II, 282–296, 325–326, 331; Arredondo, chapter 6, par. 19;
Ga. Hist. Soc. Collections, VII, Pt. I, no. I, p. 7 (Savannah, 1909).
For reports of the Georgia-Florida coast made by Arredondo after
his visit to San Simón, and for his relations with Oglethorpe in
1736, see Philip Lee Phillips, *The Lowery Collection* (Washington, 1912), 270–275. John Wesley in his journal, mentions the
visit of Arredondo to San Simón (Nehemiah Curnock, *The
Journal of The Rev. John Wesley, A.M.*, I, 267. London, 1909).

final settlement by the royal courts, but meanwhile Oglethorpe agreed to withdraw Fort St. George from St. Georges Island (San Juan). Oglethorpe regarded the treaty as a good bargain for England. Spain emphatically agreed with him, and Sánchez, who signed the document, was called home and hanged.[1]

Oglethorpe now returned to England to demand of the Trustees more soldiers, more funds, and more power.[2] The Trustees turned to Parliament and that body complied. Oglethorpe was made commander-in-chief of all

[1] The text of the treaty with Sánchez is in Harris, *Complete Collection of Voyages and Travels* (London, 1748), II, 331–332. Dempsey concluded two treaties. One was ratified by Sánchez, the other by the Junta de Guerra at San Agustín (*Ga. Col. Rec.*, I, 266). Concerning the fate of Sánchez it is stated "That the late Spanish Govern^r of Augustine who made the Treaty of Neutrality some years ago with Genl Oglethorpe, and had been therefore sent home in chains by the succeeding Govr on that account, is hang'd; and that Capt Dempsy's brother an Officer in the Spanish service is cashier'd because the Captain assisted Oglethorpe in concluding that Treaty." (*Ga. Col. Rec.*, vol. V, 351); see also Egmont's *Diary*, II, 326, 410. For the complaints against Sánchez see Brooks, *The Unwritten History of Old St. Augustine*, 156–162. Among numerous charges the treaty with Oglethorpe is not mentioned.

[2] For Oglethorpe's demands for troops and money while in England in 1737, see Stevens, *History of Georgia*, I, 150–152; Jones, *History of Georgia*, I, ch. 17; Egmont's *Diary*, II, 339, 368, 383, 401, 414–417, 427–431, 433–438, 457, 469, 494, 501; *Ga. Col. Rec.*, I, 323–324; IV, 140–151; V, 18–19.

the forces of Carolina as well as of Georgia. He was now in effect Count of the Southern March.

At this militant gesture Spain protested in still louder tones.[1] Indeed, she prepared to "reannex all that formerly belonged to the Spanish monarchy." Governor Montiano sent agents among the Creeks.[2] Four hundred soldiers were dispatched to Florida, and fresh

[1] For Geraldino's two memorials, 1736, 1737, Newcastle's reply, and the reaction of the Trustees of Georgia, see Egmont's *Diary*, II, 300–304, 426–438; Coxe, *Memoirs of Walpole*, IV, p. 9. Stevens, *History of Georgia*, I, 148–149; Wright, *Memoir*, ch. 10; Arredondo, ch. 6, par. 33 and following; Temperley, "The Causes of the War of Jenkins' Ear, 1739" (*Royal Historical Society Transactions, Third Series*, vol. III, 197–236). Montiano aided the Spanish diplomats with documents at San Agustín bearing on the "right and title of Your Majesty to the colonies illegally occupied by the English." Among other things was a map based on the knowledge of persons acquainted with the coast (*Ga. Hist. Soc. Col.*, VII, Part III, 16–18. Savannah, 1913).

[2] For Spanish war preparations in 1737 and early in 1738, see the correspondence of Montiano and Güemes, *Ga. Hist. Soc. Collections*, VII, Part I, pp. 8–20; Stevens, *History of Georgia*, I, 150–151; Clowes, *The Royal Navy, a History*, vol. III (London, 1898), p. 50; *Georgia Colonial Records*, XXII, Part I, 134–136, 217, 219, 223; Egmont, *Diary*, II, 446–447. For English war preparations at the same time, see Egmont, *Diary*, II. On February 10, 1737–8, Sir Chas. Wager (Admiral) instructed Capt. Chas. Brown at Jamaica to protect Georgia from a Spanish attack. (Ford, W. C., *Vernon-Wager Manuscripts*, 53, Washington, 1904); Arredondo, maps and reports listed in Phillips, *The Lowery Collection*, 270–275.

contingents were assembled at Havana. Seven thousand men and sixty warships were made ready there. Georgia seemed doomed, when suddenly, on March 21, Güemes received a hurried order to suspend the expedition while the two crowns deliberated over the boundary.

Walpole had stilled for the moment the fears of the Spanish court. The peaceful news was proclaimed through the streets of old San Agustín by beat of drum. But Spain's confidence had been misplaced. Oglethorpe blustered and had his way. Was Georgia to be abandoned? He got the ears of the King, and was given a regiment. Now he could hold his ground. Spain's golden moment was lost.[1]

[1] For the armed truce on the border in 1738–1739, see Stevens, *History of Georgia*, I, 150–153; Jones, *History of Georgia*, I, ch. 17. *Ga. Col. Rec.*, XXII, Part II, 68; "Relacion del Yndio Juan Ignacio de los Reyes Vecino del Pueblo de Pocatalaca." (A. G. I., 86–6–5; printed in Serrano y Sanz, 260–264); *Ga. Hist. Soc. Col.*, VII, Part I, 26–27; Brooks, *The Unwritten History of Old St. Augustine*, 175–180. The subjects treated in this chapter and the next are sketched in Chapter XIII of Robert Greenhow's rare book, *The History of Florida, Louisiana, Texas, and California, and of the adjoining countries, including the whole valley of the Mississippi, from the discovery to their incorporation with the United States of America.* Volume I. (New York, 1856.) One of the very few existing copies of this work is in the Bancroft Library.

CHAPTER VI

THE WAR OF JENKINS' EAR
(1739–1742)

The Georgia question was only one of two main bones of contention between Spain and England. Indeed, it was the smaller bone of the two. The other was a matter of trade and sea power. But both were questions of the Caribbean and its perimeter. Since the time of Hawkins, Englishmen had smuggled right and left in Spanish American waters. Then, by the Treaty of Utrecht the South Sea Company was granted legal right to a limited amount of trade in Spanish America. This privilege the company brazenly abused, and other English merchants continued to smuggle as of yore. Spain, weary of protest, established a rigorous coast guard. She freely exercised the "right of search," and captured scores of British vessels. Herein, too, abuses occurred. The blame was two-sided, of course.

The wails of the British merchants resounded throughout the realm. Parliament held a fiery debate on Spanish depredations. Robert Jenkins, one of the plaintiffs, caused a sensation. Seven years before, off Florida, a Spanish coast guard had boarded his ship, cut off one of his ears and handed it back.[1] As Exhibit No. 1 Jenkins now showed the bottled ear in Parliament. Some say that Jenkins lied. Be that as it may, his story caught the crowd and they demanded war. The excitement made Oglethorpe's muster easy, and in July he departed for Georgia. At the same time Haddock was sent with a squadron to the Mediterranean. Spain realized that she had been duped by peace talk. She protested

[1] April 30 (May 11), 1735, Geraldino directed to the Royal Asiento Company a proposal for disposing of their West Indian trade (Ford, W. C., *Vernon-Wager Manuscripts*, Washington, 1904, p. 46). For the complaints of English merchants, see *Trevor MSS.*, in *Hist. MSS. Commission Report*, XIV, App. pt. IX (London, 1895), 13–14, 24; Egmont's *Diary*, II, 440–442, 448, 474; Cobbett, *Parliamentary History of England* (London, 1812), X, 562–787; Coxe, W., *Memoirs of the Life and Administration of Sir Robert Walpole*, IV (London, 1816), p. 11. For English war steps early in 1738, see Temperley, Harold W. V., "The Causes of the War of Jenkins' Ear, 1739," in *Royal Historical Society Transactions*, Third Series, vol. III (London, 1909), 201–207, 210, 211, 213, 214; Egmont, *Diary*, II, 486, 503; Laughton, J. K., "Jenkins' Ear," in *English Historical Review*, IV (London, 1889), 743.

these new war preparations and revived her own. In America, Georgia and Florida again were likewise the scene of military activities.

But once more the tide of war was stemmed by diplomacy. War might destroy more trade than it would conquer; and Newcastle was not sure of England's claim to Georgia. In January, 1739, the Convention of El Pardo was signed.[1] Spain agreed to pay certain indemnities. All difficulties concerning "commerce and navigation in America and Europe and the limits of Florida and Carolina" were referred to a joint commission. So important was the Carolina boundary question that it was given a separate article. It provided that pending the settlement the *status quo* was to be maintained on the frontier.

The Convention of El Pardo was destined to failure. The Georgia Trustees, fearing

---

[1] For the negotiation of the Convention of El Pardo, see Temperley, "Causes of the War of Jenkins' Ear," *loc. cit.*, 214–225; Cobbett, *Parliamentary History of England*, X, 666, 957, 1023, 1028, *note;* Smollett, *The History of England*, III, 332–352 (London, 1811); *Trevor MSS.*, pp. 18–20, 24; Calvo, *Tratados*, Vol. II (Paris, 1862), 225–241; *Hare MSS.*, in *Hist. MSS. Commission, Report*, XIV, App. pt. IX (London, 1895), pp. 242–244. For the protest of the Georgia Trustees over the Convention, see Cobbett, *op. cit.*, X, 1056, 1179, 1184, 1204, 1257; *Trevor MSS.*, p. 26; *Ga. Col. Rec.*, V, 88, 97–98, 100–101, 104, 107, 113, 116–122, 125–137; Stevens, *History of Georgia*, I, 159–160.

that their province might be sacrificed, bombarded Walpole with demands for protection, and he promised it with a manly oath. "Sr Robert hearing this, call'd to Col. Bladen, and ask'd him whether England had a right to Georgia? yes, reply'd the Col' Can you prove it, said Sr Robert, and will you undertake it? the Col' answer'd he would. Then, said Sr Robert, By G—d the Spaniards shall not have it." Under further pressure the Trustees forced Walpole to defend England's "possessions" as well as her "rights" in America. This confession that the two were not identical was not lost on the Spanish diplomats. Egmont wrote in his Diary: "But when they saw that the Convention would pass, they obliged Sir Robert Walpole to put the word 'possession' into the address [to the Commons], which was of the greatest service for defeating the ensuing treaty with Spain, because thereby the Ministry were tied down from giving up an inch of ground to the Spaniards, which they have declared unless they are allowed to have restored to them, they will never make a treaty." [1]

[1] Egmont's *Diary*, III (1923), 33; Egmont's *Journal* (*Ga. Col. Rec.*, V), 120–131.

Map of the Debatable Land, 1670–1763.

In spite of bluster there was still talk of adjustment. Report had it that the king of Spain would sooner part with his capital than with Georgia. Geraldino denied the rumor and even suggested that his master might compromise on the Altamaha as a boundary. Seizing on the suggestion, Egmont went a step further and proposed that the region south of the Altamaha be left "desert and uninhabited." Geraldino then receded from his position. Nevertheless, Newcastle followed up the idea of a neutral ground. In his instructions to Keene of the Commission (April, 1739) he proposed that the San Juan be the legal boundary, but that the district between the San Juan and the Altamaha be left "unbuilt and uninhabited by Spaniards or English." [1]

The commissioners had not the ghost of a show. [2] While they deliberated the English

[1] *Ga. Col. Rec.*, V, 135–137, 146, 154; Egmont's *Diary*, III, 22, 35, 45, 51.

[2] For the failure of the Convention of El Pardo and the breach between England and Spain, see Temperley, *op. cit.*, 222–235; *Hare MSS.*, 247–248; John Morley, *Walpole* (London, 1909), 218; Coxe, William, *Memoirs of the Life and Administration of Sir Robert Walpole*, IV, 57–126, 383–389 (London, 1816); Goodrich, C. A., *Select British Eloquence* (New York, 1852), 77–79; Clowes, *The Royal Navy*, III, 51–52; *South Carolina Historical Society*

public cried for war. Instead of recalling
Haddock from the Mediterranean, the ministry built more ships and impressed more
seamen. Thereupon Spain suspended the
Asiento and refused to pay the promised
indemnity unless Haddock were recalled.[1]
In June the break came. Sealed orders were
hurried to Jamaica and the mainland colonies,
authorizing privateers to "commit all sorts of
hostilities against the Spaniards." The four-
year struggle which followed got its ridiculous
name from Jenkins' severed ear. When war
was openly declared the English mobs went
wild. Walpole, the pacifist, looked on in
alarm. "Ah!" he exclaimed, "they are ringing the bells to-day; they will soon be wringing
their hands!"

Collections, II, 270; Hart, F. R., *Admirals of the Caribbean*
(Boston, 1922), *note*, 131–132. For the protest of the king of
Spain in 1739 against British war preparations and France's
declaration that she must stand by Spain, see Smollett, *History
of England*, III, 350–352 (London, 1811); Egmont's *Diary*, III,
p. 81. The causes of the War of Jenkins' Ear are discussed by
Hertz, G. B., *British Imperialism in the Eighteenth Century*, ch.
II ("The War Fever of 1739"), London, 1908.

[1] On April 12, 1740, the King ordered Montiano to maintain
good relations with the French "during the present war," and
to call on them for supplies and munitions (A. G. I., 87–6–18);
on May 25, 1740, he ordered the viceroy of New Spain to give all
possible aid to Florida (A. G. I., 61–2–21). For Spanish de-

While the war clouds gathered in Europe,[1] Oglethorpe prepared the back country. There the struggle of traders and diplomats had been unceasing. French and Spanish agents both did their level best to keep the Indians stirred up against the English. Oglethorpe needed a strong cordon of allies in the west. The Chickasaws were devoted to the Anglomen; the Choctaws had always been French partisans. By a triumph of diplomacy, part of the Choctaws now turned against the French and opened trade with the Georgians. The Creeks were a wavering factor, and they occupied strategic ground between the European rivals.[2] Nothing but a personal visit by Oglethorpe would hold them in line, and he decided to make the journey. Chiefs Chisla-

fensive measures, see Sister Mary Frances Read, "The Viceregal Administration of Don Pedro Cebrián y Agustín, Conde de Fuenclara, 1742–1746," ch. II. (M.A. thesis, University of California, MS.); El Conde de Montijo, Representaciones sobre asuntos a la defensa colonial, Madrid, January 2, 1740 (A. G. I., 142–1–12); Castilla de Aysa, Testimonio de las Diligencias practicadas con motivo de la guerra con los Ingleses, Guadalajara, June 3, 1740 (A. G. I., 103–5–25).

[1] For England's sending sealed orders for reprisals to America, see *Hare MSS.*, 247–248; *Ga. Col. Rec.*, IV, 407, 412, 416, 419; *S. C. Hist. Soc. Col.*, II, 270; *Acts of the Privy Council, Colonial Series (1720–1745)*, III, 636 (Hereford, 1910).

[2] *Ga. Col. Rec.*, XXII, Part II, 68,95; Egmont's *Diary*, III, 80, 93.

caliche (Chigilly) and Malachee arranged for a meeting at Coweta. Upper and Lower Creeks, Chickasaws, and the friendly Choctaws promised to attend.

In July (1739) Oglethorpe ascended the Savannah to Euchie Town. Thence with an escort of rangers, traders, and Indians he set forth overland. On the way Indian hunters provided venison, wild honey, turkey, and buffalo meat. Horses and riders swam the streams. The packs were towed over in leather canoes carried for the purpose. Outside of Coweta, Indian boys and girls greeted the visitors with presents of fowls, venison, pumpkins, potatoes and watermelons. "King" Chislacaliche himself came forth bearing the English flag, and escorted the White Chief to the public square, where populace and dogs gave noisy welcome.[1] Oglethorpe met the chiefs in solemn council; a few days later they reassembled at Casista, across the river. At

[1] For Oglethorpe's journey to Coweta, see *Ga. Col. Rec.*, IV, 371–372; XXII, Pt. II, 166–167, 179, 208, 214–215; "A Ranger's Report of Travels with General Oglethorpe, 1739–1742," in Newton D. Mereness, *Travels in the American Colonies*, 215–222; Henry Bruce, *Life of General Oglethorpe* (New York, 1890), 207–208; Stephens, *Journal* (*Ga. Col. Rec.*, IV, 368–369); *Ga. Hist. Soc. Col.*, III (Savannah, 1873), 80, 87; Stevens, *History of Georgia*, I, 157–158; Wright, *Memoir*, ch. 12; Egmont's *Diary*, III, 121.

the end of ten days the Creeks renewed their
alliance with England and declared that no
Spaniard should settle north of the San Juan
River and Apalache. On August 25 Ogle-
thorpe set out for home. Eight days later he
reached Augusta. There he learned that
England and Spain were in a state of war.
His treaty with the Creeks was well timed.

This was an American war. It was
directed almost exclusively at Spain's commerce and her colonies. The main target was
the Caribbean area, with Havana at the
center and Puerto Bello, Cartagena and San
Agustín on the perimeter. Vice-Admiral
Vernon—"Old Grog," his seamen called him—
was given the center of the naval stage.[1]

[1] For Vernon's operations early in the war, see Clowes, *The
Royal Navy*, III, 51–52, 58, 67, 265–267. For the participation
of the North American troops, see Hart, F. R., *Admirals of the
Caribbean*, 139–140; Temperley, H. W. V., "The Relations of
England with Spanish America, 1720–1744," *Am. Hist. Assoc.
Ann. Rep., 1911*, I, 231–237; Storer, "Admiral Vernon Medals,"
Mass. Hist. Soc. Proc., 1918–1919, vol. 52, pp. 195–196; *An
Account of the Expedition to Carthagena [1740] with Explanatory
Notes and Observations*. London, 1743. Printed for Mr. Cooper;
Original Papers Relating to the Expedition to Carthagena [1740].
London, 1744. Printed for Mr. Cooper. See also Winsor,
Narrative and Critical History, Vol. V (Boston, 1887), and the
records of the various colonies. The Vernon-Wager Manuscripts
in the Library of Congress are rich in materials for the War of
Jenkins' Ear. (Ford, W. C., *The Vernon-Wager Manuscripts*,
pp. 60–99 *passim*.)

Oglethorpe played the chief rôle on land. With a small fleet Vernon sailed to Jamaica. Thence he proceeded to the Isthmus and captured Puerto Bello. Hysterical over the victory, England encored. A medal was struck bearing the words: "Brave Vernon made us free; no search upon the seas shall be!"

Oglethorpe was instructed at first to "anoy the Spaniards." He did not need urging. Hastening to Frederica he raised a troop of mounted rangers, and sent messengers among the Indian allies to call for warriors. They promptly responded. When war was openly declared (October, 1739), Oglethorpe struck quickly.[1] Two preliminary forays and two campaigns drove the Spaniards out of forts Pupo and Picolata, and gave him control of San Juan River, to the very back door of San Agustín (January, 1740). Montiano chafed in his ancient castle there, but he could do little, for he had only 613 men, of

[1] Oglethorpe's summons to the Indians and his first movements against Florida are treated in *Ga. Col. Rec.*, IV, 424, 474, 501, 550–551, 555; *Ga. Hist. Soc. Col.*, III, 82–94, 105–108; Montiano to Güemes, January 31, 1740 (*Ga. Hist. Soc. Col.*, VII, Pt. I, 34); *S. C. Hist. Soc. Col.*, II, 270; Stephens, *Journal* (*Ga. Col. Rec.*, IV), 447, 458, 462–465, 474, 477, 483, 501; Stevens, *History of Georgia*, I, 161, 163; Mereness, *Travels*, 224–226.

whom ninety were negroes and Indians.[1] Of
Güemes at Havana he begged a squadron to
protect the capital. Six small galliots were
sent. As it turned out they saved the city.

To Oglethorpe the San Juan was only a
means to an end. Vernon had won fame by
capturing Puerto Bello; his was the task to
take San Agustín. Hurrying to Charleston he
raised 500 men under Colonel Vanderdusen;
and with Commodore Pearce he arranged for
coöperation with the coast fleet. In April he
welcomed a new contingent of Indian allies.
In all his force consisted of about 2,000 men.[2]

Early in May Oglethorpe's army crossed
the broad San Juan. Warships effectively
patrolled the coast, and forts San Diego and
Moosa were taken. But these small successes
were followed by a series of failures. An

[1] Montiano's defensive measures down to May 14 are set
forth in his correspondence with Güemes in "Letters of Montiano.
Siege of St. Augustine," *Ga. Hist. Soc. Col.*, VII, Pt. I, 7–24,
32–53. On July 30, Montiano reported the failure of Oglethorpe's attack to the viceroy. He stated that the English loss
was more than 150 men, that of the Spaniards only 16 (The
viceroy to the King, October 15, 1740. A. G. I., 61–2–21).

[2] For Oglethorpe's appeals to South Carolina, see Oglethorpe
to Bull, December 29, 1739, in Harris, *Voyages and Travels*, II,
338–340; *S. C. Hist. Soc. Col.*, II, 271; Stevens, *History of Georgia*,
I, 170; Jones, *History of Georgia*, I, 327; Wright, *Memoir of James
Oglethorpe*, 232–233, 238–243.

attempt to assault the city was frustrated by
the six galliots in the harbor. They, if any,
were the heroes in the engagement. The
English garrison left at Fort Moosa was cut
to pieces by Montiano. Oglethorpe's plan for
an assault now gave way to a siege.[1]   Bat-
teries on Santa Anastasia Island bombarded
the town, but without effect.   Starvation
promised to be a more deadly weapon, but
Spanish supply ships eluded the besiegers and
relieved the famine. The task of the English
was hopeless now, and on July 20 they raised
the siege. Oglethorpe had repeated Moore's
failure of forty years before.   In old San
Agustín there was rejoicing.

This was a war of failures. Oglethorpe's
retreat from San Agustín was followed by a
series of reverses to "Old Grog" in the Caribbean. In the summer of 1740 he was joined
by 3,500 troops from the northern mainland
colonies, and a little later by 9,000 more from
England. "A fleet such as heretofore had
never been assembled in the waters of the

[1] For English accounts of Oglethorpe's attack on San Agustín,
see Stevens, *History of Georgia*, I, 171–179; Wright, *Memoir*,
243–260; Harris, *Voyages and Travels*, II, 339–340; Jones,
History of Georgia, I, chs. 20–21.   For the Spanish version, see
Montiano's correspondence with Güemes, *Ga. Hist. Soc. Col.*, vol.
VII, Pt. I, 54–65.

Ruins on the Altamaha, opposite Darien.

New World was now at the disposal of the British commander."

It was hoped that Vernon would next attack Havana.[1] "All our hearts are bent on Cuba," Pulteney wrote him. "No search, take and hold," became the war cry. But just now Spain sent Torres to the West Indies with a powerful Spanish fleet. To take Havana was easier said than done. Vernon therefore turned to Cartagena. But a deadly climate and quarrels with Wentworth caused disaster there, and Vernon returned to Jamaica.[2] Then followed another failure. Vernon was ordered to take Havana, but Torres still blocked the way. Santiago was therefore selected as the victim instead. Gingerly Vernon looked it over. Concluding that it was impregnable by sea, he sent Wentworth to

[1] For English desire to conquer Cuba, see *Gentleman's Magazine* (London, 1748), XVIII, 303–304: *Trevor MSS.*, p. 59; Ford, *Vernon-Wager Manuscripts*, August 5, 1739, August 8, 1739, October 24, 1739; undated instructions to Admiral Wager, etc., pp. 63, 64, 68.

[2] For Vernon's movements in 1741, see Clowes, *The Royal Navy*, III, 67–75; Hart, F. R., *Admirals of the Caribbean*, 149–153, and the bibliography, 194–195. *Original Papers Relating to the Expedition to Panamá*, 1741–42, London, 1744. Printed for M. Cooper. *Original Papers Relating to the Expedition to the Island of Cuba* [1741]. London, 1744. Printed for M. Cooper. Smollett, Tobias, *History of England*, III, 381–391 (London, 1811). In his *Adventures of Roderick Random*, a novel,

attack it by land. But Wentworth lost heart in the trackless swamps, and turned back. The campaign was soon abandoned, and the fleet returned to Jamaica.

The Spaniards now assumed the aggressive. Privateers swarmed the Caribbean waters and played havoc with English commerce. From Georgia to New York they terrorized the northern mainland coast. Carolina and Georgia plantations were sacked.[1] Within the year ending August, 1741, more than thirty English prizes were taken into the harbor of San Agustín alone.

Oglethorpe had no intention of quitting. Instead he proposed a new drive on San Agustín and made preparations for putting it through. The ministry were favorable and the drive was planned for March (1742).

Smollett wrote a brief account of the expedition against Cartagena, in which he took part as an army surgeon. He wrote a longer account in his *Compendium of Voyages* (London, 1756). For Spanish reprisals, from September, 1739, to November, 1741, see Clowes, *op. cit.*, III, 264–265. For plans for the Spanish campaign against Georgia and Carolina, see the correspondence and instructions in *Ga. Hist. Soc. Col.*, VII, Pt. III, 20–47; Ford, W. C., *Vernon-Wager Manuscripts*, 87–100, *passim*.

[1] For the sacking of Carr's plantation in 1741, see Egmont's *Journal* (*Ga. Col. Rec.*, V), 484, 529. For Spanish captures, see *Ga. Col. Rec.*, IV, supplement (Atlanta, 1908), 117, 223–224; *ibid.*, VI, 370; Clowes, *The Royal Navy*, III, 264–265.

But money was short, red tape long, and
dissension debilitating.[1] Critics carped. The
Trustees were grafters, they said, and Georgia
was not worth a war. Sir John Cotton was so
bold as to urge in Parliament that Port Royal
be made the boundary, as Spain demanded.
The Trustees finally triumphed. Georgia was
declared useful to England, and Stephens, the
chief critic of the Trustees, was publicly
humiliated.[2] Vindicated, Egmont rejoiced
that his enemy would be "brought to his
marrow-bones." On June 30, 1742, the luck-
less young Stephens, in full view of Parliament,
bent one knee before his accusers. This was
not enough. "Both knees," demanded the

[1] For Oglethorpe's proposal of another campaign against
San Agustín, May, 1741, see *Ga. Col. Rec.*, V, 553. For Carr's
arrival with Maryland marines, see *ibid.*, V, 511. For Dunbar's
mission to raise Indians, see Wright, *A Memoir of General James
Oglethorpe* (London, 1867), 279–281. For the conference with
Chief Wolf, see *Ga. Col. Rec.*, IV, supplement, 160, 162, 173.

[2] For discussion in England of the value of Georgia and of
plans for a campaign, see *Ga. Col. Rec.*, IV, supplement, 234,
253, 275; *Ga. Col. Rec.*, V, 273, 293–313, 355, 416, 422, 430,
432–436, 489, 496–498, 514–555 (settlers for Georgia), 560, 561,
565, 575–579, 589, 592, 601, 611, 612, 619, 620, 633, 635–636,
637–644; Wright, *Memoir*, 280; *Ga. Col. Rec.*, XXIII, 459. For
proposals of Harman Verelst and Oglethorpe, concerning the
war in Georgia and Florida, and proceedings thereon by the Lords
Commissioners of Trade and Plantations, October 15-November
20, 1741, see Ford, *Vernon-Wager Manuscripts*, 98–99.

Speaker; and both joints were flexed for half
an hour. The Trustees gloated to witness
their critic's degradation. But England's
chance to take the offensive had passed, for
Spain had assumed that position.

In October the Spanish ministry had
decided to launch an expedition to drive the
English out of Georgia, and make good
Spain's claims as far as Port Royal.[1] They
would regain by war what had been lost by
pacifism and the deceptive Convention of El
Pardo. Now was the opportune moment.
Vernon's failure at Santiago released Torres
somewhat from his arduous watch at Havana.
England's northern colonies were weakened by
the drain of Vernon's futile expeditions.

In anticipation of victory, perhaps, Arredondo in Havana sat down and wrote an
"Historical Proof of the right of the Catholic
King to the territory held to-day by the
British king under the name of New Georgia
in the provinces and Continent of Florida, by
which is proved the unquestionable title of
the King of Spain as far as north latitude 32°
30' inclusive, where lies the harbor of the

---

[1] For Montiano's proposal for a counter blow, July 28, 1740,
see *Ga. Hist. Soc. Col.*, VII, Pt. I, pp. 62–64.

island of Santa Elena." This was the line which the campaign must establish.

Güemes was entrusted with preparations. Havana was made the base of supplies and convoy ships. Montiano was put at the head of the expedition, with Rubiani in charge of the fleet and second in command.[1] The expedition was designed to expel the English from Georgia and to devastate South Carolina. It must "inflict a damage that will ruin and terrify them. It must burn all towns, posts, plantations and settlements." It must repay the attacks of Drake, Moore, and Oglethorpe. Above all it must recover Georgia.

Two Spanish diaries tell us what happened.[2] One of them was written by Arredondo. On June 1 a flotilla of ten small vessels left Havana. Five days later the main fleet set sail. At San Agustín the vessels reassembled and took on the Florida contingent. Now for a few days the old harbor presented a lively scene. Busiest of

[1] A Spanish view of Montiano's campaign against Georgia is contained in "The Spanish Official Account of the Attack on the Colony of Georgia in America, and of its Defeat on St. Simons Island by General James Oglethorpe," in *Ga. Hist. Soc. Col.*, Vol. VII, Part III (Savannah, 1913), pp. 20–108.

[2] These are the diaries of Montiano and Casinas (*ibid.*, 52–87).

all was Arredondo, chief-of-staff. When all was ready it was an imposing force that stood out to sea. The fleet consisted of fifty vessels carrying eighteen hundred soldiers and about a thousand seamen.

The main Georgia targets were St. Simons and Frederica. These destroyed, the fleet would continue by the Inland Passage to Savannah and Port Royal. The first day out from San Agustín the vessels were scattered by a storm. Oglethorpe rushed down the coast to meet the Spaniards, and their attacks on Fort St. Andrews and Fort William failed. Returning to Frederica Oglethorpe assembled his troops and organized a fleet in the harbor of Gualquini.[1]

For six days Montiano was prevented by a storm from entering that bay. On the sixteenth he forced an entrance in the face of fire from forts and flotilla. It was a bold enterprise, such as Oglethorpe had tried in vain at San Agustín. Oglethorpe retreated

[1] For Oglethorpe's preparations, see Wright, Robert, *A Memoir of General James Oglethorpe* (London, 1867), pp. 293–300; Stevens, *History of Georgia*, I, 180–184; Jones, *History of Georgia*, I, 341–346; *Ga. Col. Rec.*, III, 131–132; XXIII, 409, 438; Jones, C. C., *The Dead Towns of Georgia* (Savannah, 1878), 102–105.

to Frederica; his fleet dispersed. The invaders
landed and occupied the forts and village of
St. Simons.[1]

Montiano planned next to advance on
Frederica, and two detachments were sent
out to learn the trails. The only road to
Frederica was a narrow path cut through the
woods along the edge of a great marsh. The
men had to go single file, but they managed
to get within two miles of the town. Oglethorpe leaped on a horse, led out Highlanders,
Rangers and Indians, and rushed to the spot.
The Spaniards, defeated, fled in confusion.
Montiano hurried three companies of gren-
adiers to cover the retreat. With shouts and
drum beat they advanced to the marsh and
halted within a hundred paces of some of
Oglethorpe's men in ambush. Stacking arms,
they kindled fires and prepared to cook a meal.
It was gross carelessness. Suddenly they were
set upon and routed. Many fled without
their muskets, others were left dead on the
field. In the two engagements the Spanish

[1] Diaries of Arredondo and Casinas, *Ga. Hist. Soc. Col.*, VII,
Pt. III, 53–64, 65–69; Montiano's reports, *ibid.*, 48–49, 88–91;
Wright, *Memoir*, 302–303. *Ga. Hist. Soc. Col.*, III, 125, 140–141,
143–145. For a manuscript copy of Arredondo's diary, see
Phillips, *The Lowery Collection*, 273–274.

loss was two hundred. These combats are famed in Georgia history as the Battle of Bloody Marsh.[1]

The tide of war had turned. Montiano tried to effect a landing at Frederica by the river but was driven back. Oglethorpe in turn attempted a night assault but was betrayed by a French deserter. Next day Spanish lookouts in the masts reported an English fleet approaching from the north. Fearing attack by both land and sea, the Spaniard hurriedly retreated to San Agustín.[2] Oglethorpe and Montiano were now even. The Boston rhymster wrote, in January, 1743:

> From Georgia to Augustine the General goes;
> From Augustine to Georgia come our foes;
> Hardy from Charleston to St. Simons hies,
> Again from thence to Charleston back he flies.
> Forth from St. Simons then the Spaniards creep;
> "Say Children, Is not this your Play, Bo Peep?"

[1] For the Battle of Bloody Marsh, see Casinas's diary, *loc. cit.*, 72; Montiano's report, *ibid.*, 91–92. Stevens, *History of Georgia*, I, ch. 5; Jones, *History of Georgia*, I, ch. 22; Wright, *Memoir*, ch. 16; Jones, C. C., *The Dead Towns of Georgia*, 107–115.

[2] For events after the defeat at Bloody Marsh, see Wright, *Memoir*, 308–312; Casinas, *Ga. Hist. Soc. Col.*, VII, Pt. III, 76–87; Montiano, *ibid.*, 94; Jones, *Dead Towns of Georgia*, 110–113.

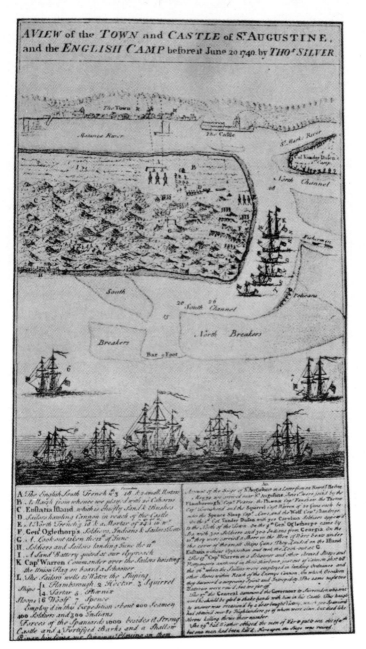

The Siege of San Augustín.   By Thomas Silver.

In recognition of his "good service in repulsing the Spaniards from Frederica" Oglethorpe was made Brigadier General.[1] In July, 1743, he sailed for England, never to return. He was a conquering hero, and was cleared of all charges against him. Years later, when an old man, he had a tale to tell. To Oliver Goldsmith, Sir Joshua Reynolds, and other boon companions, he spun yarns of adventure in Georgia, and furnished Goldsmith inspiration for the lines:

> Through torrid tracts, with fainting steps they go,
> Where wild Altama murmurs to their woe.

[1] For Oglethorpe's promotions, see *Ga. Col. Rec.*, V, 679; Wright, *Memoir*, 325, 331, 336, 337, 345; *Ga. Hist. Soc. Col.*, III, 146; Jones, *History of Georgia*, I, ch. 22.

CHAPTER VII

THE NEUTRAL GROUND AND THE FINAL STRUGGLE

(1743–1763)

For several years now the country south of the Altamaha continued to be what Newcastle had suggested, an "uninhabited tract." England maintained Fort William on Cumberland Island and another small post on Jekyl Island. For a short time Carr had a plantation on Blythe Island and Heron another near by. But through continued raids from the south these plantations were abandoned, and the slender island posts alone remained.[1]

Though "deserted and unbuilt," the region remained debatable ground. Legally speaking, nothing had been settled by the war. Neither side relinquished its claim. Spain continued to stand on the treaty of 1670. Indeed, she appealed to France to make it good. France responded. By the treaty of Fontainebleau (1743) she pledged herself to

[1]For posts on Cumberland and Jekyl, see *Ga. Col. Rec.*, XXV, 396–397; XXVI, 28–31.

"oblige the English to destroy the new colony of Georgia and all forts built on Spanish soil."[1] France entered the colonial war, but she failed to keep her promise regarding Georgia.   Attention in the struggle was now turned to the north.   The St. Lawrence supplanted the Caribbean; Cape Breton overshadowed Havana and San Agustín.

As the war dragged on various peace proposals were made.   One provided for a commission to try once more to settle the Carolina boundary.   Spain again demanded that Georgia be evacuated, and rumors got abroad that this might come to pass.   Frightened, Oglethorpe and other Trustees appealed to the Duke of Bedford.   The fear was groundless, for the treaty of Aix-la-Chapelle restored everything to the *status quo ante bellum*.   War being over, the Georgia regiment was now disbanded; but some sixty men were kept at the island posts, "as a sign of possession."   By England the opposite mainland south of the

[1] For the treaty of Fontainebleau, see Cantillo, *Tratados, Convenios, y Declaraciones de Paz y de Comercio* (Madrid, 1843), 370; Lucien Schöne, *La Politique Coloniale Sous Louis XV et Louis XVI* (Paris, 1907), 119–121; Forbonnais, *Histoire et Commerce des Colonies Anglaises*, p. 327 (London, 1755), cited by Schöne.

Altamaha was treated as Neutral Ground.[1]
Pending an adjustment it must be left unoccupied.

For a decade now England toyed with this
idea of a Neutral Ground. Nonchalantly Spain
let her toy. The peace of 1748 was only a
truce, and both England and France com-
peted for the good will of Spain. England must
not offend her unnecessarily by an invasion
of disputed territory. The Court of Madrid
was also in a conciliatory mood. By a new
treaty Spain and England made mutual con-
cessions (1750). Spain yielded to English
merchants extensive privileges. In return the
Asiento of the South Sea Company was terminated. The treaty was ordered published in
Georgia with a warning to "avoid giving the
least ground for such complaint as may, in
any wise, interrupt the good Harmony . . .
between the two Crowns."

[1] For peace movements in 1745, see *Trevor MSS.*, 122–129.
For the proposal of 1747, see Lord John Russell, *Correspondence
of John, Fourth Duke of Bedford* (three vols. London, 1842–1846),
I, 288–330. For French insistence on the abrogation of the Asiento,
see Russell, *Correspondence of Bedford*, I, 448, 451, 476, 477,
528–536. For the fear felt by the Trustees, see *Ga. Col. Rec.*, I,
508–510. For the peace of 1748, see Chalmers, *Collection of
Treaties*, vol. I; Russell, *Correspondence of Bedford*, I, 273–287,
391, 586–588.

But old animosities could not be entirely forgotten in a minute. Georgia settlers felt uneasy and called for a garrison on the Altamaha (1751). Disturbing reports were heard of new fortifications at San Agustín and San Marcos; Spain's minister Ensenada showed a French leaning. Hostile orders were sent to the Spanish governors; and Spanish agents showed suspicious activity among the Lower Creeks. Bedford complained. Yielding, the King of Spain repudiated the objectionable orders, dismissed Ensenada, and put Ricardo Wall in his place. Anglo-Spanish relations were greatly improved by the change, and, though France and England again went to war, Spain remained neutral (1755).[1]

But just when Spain's friendship was most important it was threatened by a violation of the Neutral Ground. Unruly frontiersmen crossed the Altamaha without permission.

[1] For English desire to conciliate Spain after 1748, see Russell, *Correspondence of Bedford*, II, 31, 34–35, 45, 46, 58, 70–72; *Ga. Col. Rec.*, XXVI, 149. For the treaty of 1750, see Cantillo, *Tratados*, 409–410. For trade relations between Florida and Georgia after 1750, see *Ga. Col. Rec.*, VIII, 347, 594, 687–90. For border fears, animosities, and Indians raids after 1750, see *Ga. Col. Rec.*, I, 560; VI, 417, 421, 440–442, 451; VII, 390–401, 420–425. For Ensenada's hostile policy, see Russell, *Correspondence of Bedford*, II, 71–72, 151, 152, 154; Yorke, *The Life and Correspondence of Philip Yorke, Earl of Hardwicke, Lord High Chancellor of Great Britain* (Cambridge, 1913, 3 vols.), III, 251.

Malcontents from Augusta and the Ogeechee settlements, "runagates" from Carolina and Virginia, these men were called. Headed by Edmund Gray they had opposed Governor Reynolds in politics. He had the whip hand, and they were expelled from the Georgia Assembly on the charge of sedition. Some of them sought liberty in the Neutral Ground. There, on Satilla River, thirty miles from its mouth, "Gray's Gang" formed a settlement called New Hanover, and engaged in Indian trade. Ephraim Alexander opened a store and trading post. Fearful of consequences, Reynolds visited the border (April, 1755). He was not reassured by what he saw. With alarm he wrote that the emigrants were going south "by boats full." His commission gave him authority only to the Altamaha. The Satilla was in the Neutral Ground. But in the interest of good order Reynolds asked the Board of Trade to extend his rule to the St. Marys. For good reasons his petition was denied. Spain's policy was uncertain and the Creeks complained of Gray's Gang. Both Spaniards and Indians must be kept friendly.[1]

[1] For Reynolds and Gray's Gang, see *Ga. Col. Rec.*, VI, 425, 441; VII, 95, 100, 171, 173, 252, 294, 333; Stevens, *History of Georgia*, I, 405-407, 412-413; Jones, *History of Georgia*, I, 486-487.

Spanish reaction to the colony on the Satilla was not long left in doubt. A force of thirty-four men was sent from San Agustín to New Hanover (October, 1756). The captain bore a document which, being written in Spanish, Gray could not read. But he understood the verbal orders that the intruders must withdraw from Spanish soil; and he promised to refer the matter to his governor. For three days the Spaniards visited amicably, traded at Alexander's store, and then departed.[1]

Reynolds was succeeded by Ellis. One of the new governor's first acts was to visit the southern frontier and confer with Gray, early in 1757. There he was apprised of a new danger. The Spanish governor was now trying to attract Gray's Gang to his own standard. Gray informed Ellis that Alexander had been urged to move his trading post to the north bank of the San Juan under Spanish protection. This would be a recognition of Spain's authority in the disputed area. It would be better, the shrewd Gray suggested, for Ellis himself to issue a license, as a sign of

[1] For Gray's visit to "St. Taffeys" and Spanish reaction to Gray's Gang, see *Ga. Col. Rec.*, VII, 425–430, 451, 477, 480; Stevens, *History of Georgia*, I, 437–439.

England's authority. As a compromise Alexander was permitted to establish a post on the St. Marys opposite Fort William.[1] Across the channel on Cumberland Island another settlement was now formed. These "profligate and refractory" intruders were suspected of having received encouragment from the government of Florida to settle there, in conjunction with a number of Spanish families "sent thither from their islands, purposely to establish a colony in those regions."

Ellis had made a *faux pas*. He had violated the Neutral Ground. The Board of Trade vigorously denounced his act. The settlement on the Satilla was "an open defiance of his Majesty's lawful authority." The settlers' influence with the Indians was dangerous. Moreover, it might "disturb that

[1] For Ellis and the Indians, see *Ga. Col. Rec.*, VII, 179–180, 206, 251–261, 294, 492, 494, 539, 540, 546, 643–667, 703–706; Stevens, *History of Georgia*, I, 412, 422–423, 427, 439, 440–443. For Ellis's relations with Gray's Gang and with the Spaniards, see *Ga. Col. Rec.*, VII, 544, 547, 548; Stevens, *History of Georgia*, I, 437–438; Jones, *History of Georgia*, I, 531, 539. On August 26, 1756, the governor of Florida reported Braddock's defeat to the viceroy of Mexico and added that the Indians were peaceful and that he was perfecting the forts at San Agustín and San Marcos. (A. G. I., 86–6–6.) In July, 1759, Governor Palacios reported Creek (Uchis) hostilities against the Spaniards (A. G. I., 86–6–6.); in 1761 the western Creeks attacked Pensacola (A. G. I., 89–3–15 and 89–3–13).

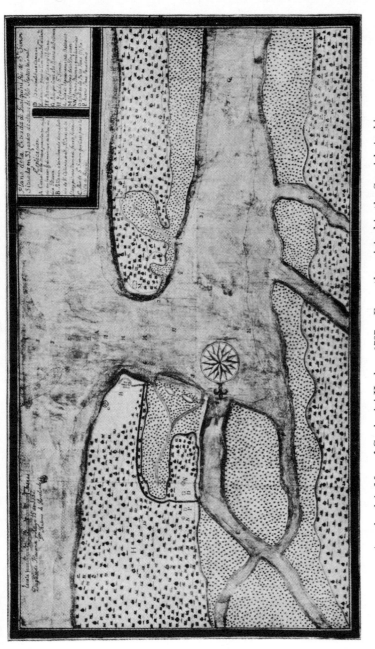

Arredondo's Map of Gualquini Harbor, 1737.   From the original in the Spanish Archives.

peace and friendship which at present so happily subsists between his Majesty and the King of Spain, no limits having, as we apprehend, ever been settled between the two crowns in that part of America." The St. Marys was not in Ellis' jurisdiction; and the licensing of Alexander to establish a post there might be considered by Spain as a declaration of England's right to the land.[1]

The Board of Trade referred the matter to Pitt, and the New Hanover settlers were ordered "to remove immediately from thence" (June 10, 1758). Government had spoken, and there was pretended compliance. Early in 1759 commissioners served notice on the settlers, and by March they had departed. But the troublesome frontiersmen "did only make a show or appearance of so doing, and immediately returned back to their settlements." There they still were two years later.[2]

[1] For official correspondence of the home government concerning Gray's Gang, see Charles Lee, *A Report of the Attorney General to Congress; containing a collection of Charters, Treaties, and other Documents Relative to and Explanatory of the Title to the Land Situate in the South Western Parts of the United States; and claimed by Certain companies Under a Law of the State of Georgia, Passed January 7, 1795* (Philadelphia, 1796), 105–111; *Ga. Col. Rec.*, VII, 844–845, VIII, 585.

[2] For the removal of Gray's Gang, see *Ga. Col. Rec.*, VII, 875–876; Stevens, *History of Georgia*, I, 448, 449.

The Satilla settlement was probably more obnoxious to the English than to the Spanish authorities. Governor Wright complained that it was used as "an Asylum by Persons who fly thither, to shelter themselves from Justice." But having no authority to use force to eject them he could only appeal to the Board.

Gray's influence with the Creeks had been regarded as a menace. Now it was put to account. In 1759 the French succeeded in turning the Cherokees against the English. To strike a counter blow Ellis fitted out a Creek war party and put Gray in command of it. In April, Gray marched into Savannah at the head of a conquering band displaying Cherokee scalps. The braves were congratulated, and richly rewarded for being the first to shed Cherokee blood. But even Gray's services did not avail him to get permission to invade the Neutral Ground. He applied for a renewal of his license to trade in the south. Governor Wright gave consent, but only on condition that the permit be restricted to Cumberland Island.[1]

[1] For Gray's service in the Cherokee War, see *Ga. Col. Rec.*, VIII, 284, 292–294, 569.

Inevitably Spain was drawn at last into the war. Her neutrality had been greatly strained by her French sympathies. In vain she had interceded on behalf of France. She felt that further neutrality was merely hastening her own destruction. Ricardo Wall, once England's zealous friend, shouted in anger to the Earl of Bristol that all the English aimed at was "to ruin the French Power, in order the more easily to crush Spain;" to drive Spain's subjects from their island colonies; and "to destroy their several Forts and Settlements on the Continent of North America." In this mood Spain renewed the Family Compact (1761); then England declared war. The fate of Georgia was now sealed.[1]

Carlos III had championed a cause already lost. Quebec had fallen before the Compact was signed. Humiliation for Spain was inevitable, and inch by inch she yielded her claims. Grimaldi at first denounced the cession of Louisiana to England; resistance being futile, he proposed a neutral zone west of the Alleghanies to keep England from the

[1] For the breach with Spain, see *Papers Relating to the Rupture with Spain Laid Before Both Houses of Parliament on Friday the Twenty-ninth Day of January, 1762, By His Majesty's command* (London, 1762).

Gulf. Next he was ready to yield Georgia,
with a "reasonable" boundary on the south—
presumably the Altamaha. Then Havana
fell, and the vise tightened. England offered
to restore Havana in exchange for Florida or
Puerto Rico. Florida could be spared better
than the island. But to cede it would give
England control of the Gulf and the Bahama
Channel, the evil Spain had so long resisted.
To save Florida for Spain, therefore, France
offered England all of Louisiana. But England preferred Florida, and took it. La
Florida was gone; with it vanished all of
Spain's claims to Georgia. Ostensibly to
compensate Spain for her loss, France now
gave Spain western Louisiana, which England
had rejected. Reluctantly she accepted it.[1]

The treaty of Paris ended the long contest
between England and Spain over the debatable land of Georgia. But it served also to
revive an old quarrel between Georgia and
Carolina. Before the treaty was ratified the
governor of South Carolina proceeded to

[1] For a discussion of the Louisiana cession, see Shepherd, in
Political Science Quarterly, XIX, 439–458. For the treaty of
Paris, February 10, 1763, see MacDonald, W., *Select Charters
and Other Documents Illustrative of American History* (New York,
1906), 261–267.

grant to Carolinians large tracts of land south of the Altamaha. Governor Wright protested. Suddenly he had become a good Spaniard. Carolina's claim to the area on the ground of the grant to 29° was ridiculous, he said. That grant took in St. Augustine, Pensacola, and Mobile [and he might have added El Paso, Santa Fé and Albuquerque], "and therefore Mr. Boone may just as well pretend a right to grant those places as any spot of land to the southward of the river Altamaha." Arredondo himself could scarcely have stated Spain's case better.[1] The home Government took the Spanish view of the question—it was safe to do so now—and denied Carolina's claim.

Our story now soon ends. Two Gulf provinces, East and West Florida, were organized from England's new acquisitions.[2] East

[1] For the controversy between Georgia and South Carolina over land grants after the treaty of 1763, see Charles Lee, *Report of the Attorney General*, 112–132; Letters of Hon. James Habersham, in *Ga. Hist. Soc. Col.*, VI, 10–15 (Savannah, 1904).

[2] For plans for the administration of the new acquisitions, see Lee, *Report of the Attorney General*, 133–136; for the Proclamation of 1763, see MacDonald, *Select Charters*, 267. The next January, by Governor Wright's commission, Georgia's north and south boundaries were extended to the Mississippi. For Governor Wright's commission, see *Certain Documents and Reports Relating to the Locating and Marking of the Line Between the Territory and State of Florida and the State of Georgia*. 60th Cong., 1st sess., Senate Doc. No. 467, (Washington, 1908).

Florida was delimited on the north by the St. Marys River, and a line thence to the forks of the Apalachicola. The strip between the St. Marys and the Altamaha was added to Georgia. It was no longer Debatable Land.

BIBLIOGRAPHY

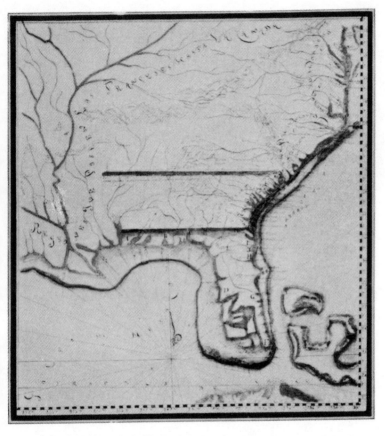

Arredondo's Map of the Debatable Land. From the original in the Spanish Archives. Through the reduction the details are lost, but the heavy parallel lines convey Arredondo's idea of the area in dispute.

BIBLIOGRAPHY

(List of printed works cited)

ABAD Y LASIERRA, DON IÑIGO. Relación de el Descubrimiento, Conquista y Población de las Provincias y Costas de la Florida. Año de 1785. In Serrano y Sanz, Documentos Históricos de La Florida y La Luisiana, Siglos XVI al XVIII. Madrid, 1912.

ALVORD, CLARENCE WALWORTH, and BIDGOOD, LEE. The first explorations of the Trans-Allegheny Region by the Virginians, 1650-1674. Cleveland, 1912.

ARREDONDO, DON ANTONIO DE. Journal kept by Don Antonio de Arredondo, Chief Engineer of the Present Expedition. Translation in Collections of the Georgia Historical Society, Vol. VII, Pt. I. Savannah, 1913.

BARCÍA, ANDRÉS GONZÁLEZ (Don Gabriel de Cárdenas Z Cano). Ensayo Cronológico, para la Historia General de la Florida. Desde el Año de 1512. Que Descubrió la Florida, Juan Ponce de León, hasta el de 1722. Escrito por Don Gabriel de Cárdenas Z Cano, Dedicado al Príncipe Nuestro Señor. Con Privilegio: En Madrid, 1723.

BARNWELL, JOSEPH W. "Dr. Henry Woodward, The First English Settler in South Carolina, and Some of his Descendants." In the South Carolina Historical and Genealogical Magazine, Vol. VIII, Charleston, 1907.

BASANIER (editor). L'Histoire Notable de la Floride située en Indes Occidentales contenant les Trois Voyages Faicts en Icelle par Certains Capitaines et Pilotes François Descrits par le Captaine Laudonière qui y a Commandé L'Espace D'un an Trois Moys. Paris, 1586. Reprinted in Paul Gaffarel, Histoire de la Floride Française. Paris, 1875.

BOLTON, HERBERT EUGENE. The Spanish Borderlands: A Chronicle of Old Florida and the Southwest. New Haven, 1921.

BOLTON, HERBERT EUGENE, and MARSHALL, THOMAS MAITLAND.
The Colonization of North America, 1492–1783. New York,
1920.

BROOKS, A. M. The Unwritten History of Old St. Augustine,
Copied from the Spanish Archives in Seville, Spain, by
Miss A. M. Brooks, and Translated by Mrs. Annie Averette.
St. Augustine, 1909?

BROWN, ALEXANDER. The First Republic in America; an
Account of the Origin of this Nation. Written from the
Records Then (1624) Concealed by the Council Rather than
From the Histories Then Licensed by the Crown. Boston,
1898.

BROWN, ALEXANDER. The Genesis of the United States. A
Narrative of the Movement in England, 1605–1616, which
Resulted in the Plantation of North America by Englishmen,
Disclosing the Contest between England and Spain for the
Possession of the Soil now Occupied by the United States of
America. By Alexander Brown. 2 vols. Boston and New
York, 1890.

BRUCE, HENRY. Life of General Oglethorpe. New York, 1890.

BUCKINGHAMSHIRE, EARL OF. The Manuscripts of the Earl of
Buckinghamshire (Trevor MSS.). In the Fourteenth Re-
port, Appendix, Part IX, of the Historical Manuscripts
Commission of Great Britain. London, 1895. See *Trevor*.

CALVO, CARLOS. Colección Completa de los Tratados, Con-
venciones, Capitulaciones, Armisticios y Otros Actos
Diplomáticos de Todos Los Estados de la América Latina
Comprendidos entre el golfo de Méjico y el cabo de Hornos,
Desde el Año de 1493 Hasta Nuestros Dias. 6 vols. Paris,
1862 (vols. 1–3); Madrid, 1864 (vols. 4–6).

CANTILLO, DON ALEJANDRO DEL. Tratados, Convenios, y
Declaraciones de Paz y de Comercio que han hecho con las
Potencias Estranjeras los Monarcas Españoles de la Casa de
Borbon. Desde el Año de 1700 Hasta el Dia. Por Don
Alejandro del Cantillo, oficial que ha sido en la Primera
Secretaría de Estado y del Despacho. Madrid, 1843.

CARROLL, B. R. Historical Collections of South Carolina; Embracing many Rare and Valuable Pamphlets, and Other Documents, Relating to the History of that State, From its First Discovery to its Independence, in the year 1776. 2 vols. New York, 1836.

CASINAS, EL MARQUÉS DE. Details of What Occurred in the Present Expedition, Entrusted to the Care of Brigadier Don Manuel de Montiano, from the 15th Day of June, on which the Convoy Arrived from Havana at St. Augustine, the Whole Being Contained in a Journal, Kept by the Marquess of Casinas, etc. Translation in Collections of the Georgia Historical Society, Vol. VII, Pt. III. Savannah, 1913.

CHALMERS, GEORGE. A Collection of Treaties between Great Britain and other Powers. 2 vols. London, 1790.

CLOWES, SIR WILLIAM LAIRD. The Royal Navy, a History from the Earliest Times to the Present; by Wm. Laird Clowes . . . Assisted by Sir Clements Markham . . . Captain A. T. Mahan, U.S.N., H. W. Wilson, Theodore Roosevelt, E. Fraser; etc. . . . 7 vols. Boston, 1897–1903.

CONNOR, JEANNETTE THURBER (translator). Pedro Menéndez de Avilés, Adelantado, Governor and Captain-General of Florida. Memorial by Gonzalo Solís de Merás. First Published in La Florida, su Conquista y Colonización por Pedro Menéndez de Avilés, by Eugenio Ruidíaz y Caravia. Deland, Florida (The Florida State Historical Society), 1923.

CORBETT, SIR JULIAN STAFFORD (editor). Papers Relating to the Navy During the Spanish War, 1585–1587. London, 1898.

COXE, WILLIAM. Memoirs of the Life and Administration of Sir Robert Walpole, Earl of Orford. 4 vols. London, 1816.

CRANE, VERNER W. "An Historical Note on the Westo Indians." In American Anthropologist, New Series, Vol. XX. Lancaster, 1918.

CRANE, VERNER W. "The Origin of the Name of the Creek Indians." In the Mississippi Valley Historical Review. Vol. V. Cedar Rapids, 1918.

CRANE, VERNER W. "The Southern Frontier in Queen Anne's War." In American Historical Review, Vol. XXIV. Washington, 1919.

CURNOCK, NEHEMIAH (editor). The Journal of the Rev. John Wesley, A.M. 8 vols. London, 1909–1916. See *Wesley*.

DÁVILA PADILLA, FRAY AVGVSTÍN. Historia de la Fvndación y Discvrso de la Provincia, de Santiago de México, de la Orden de Predicadores Por las vidas de sus varones insignes y casos Notables de Nueua España, Por el Maestro Fray Avgvstín Dávila Padilla. Al Príncipe de España, Don Felipe nuestro Señor. Edición Segvnda. En Brvsselas. En casa de Ivan de Meerbeque, MDCXXV.

DUNN, WILLIAM EDWARD. "Letter from Joseph Baily, December 12, 1672." In South Carolina Historical and Genealogical Magazine, Vol. XVIII, Charleston, 1917.

DUNN, WILLIAM EDWARD. Spanish and French Rivalry in the Gulf Region of the United States, 1678–1702: the Beginnings of Texas and Pensacola. Austin, 1917.

EGMONT, FIRST EARL OF. Manuscripts of the Earl of Egmont, Diary of the First Earl of Egmont (Viscount Percival). Historical Manuscripts Commission. 3 vols. London, 1920–1923.

EGMONT, FIRST EARL OF. Journal of the Earl of Egmont. First President of the Board of Trustees, from June 14, 1738, to May 25, 1744. In The Colonial Records of Georgia, Vol. V, Atlanta, 1908.

ENGELHARDT, FR. ZEPHYRIN, O. F. M. "Missionary Labors of the Franciscans Among the Indians of the Early Days (Florida). "In The Franciscan Herald, Vols. I–II, Chicago, 1913–1914.

FAIRBANKS, GEORGE R. History of Florida from its Discovery by Ponce de León, in 1512, to the close of the Florida War, in 1842. Philadelphia and Jacksonville, 1871.

FORCE, PETER (editor). Tracts and Other Papers, Relating Principally to the Origin, Settlement and Progress of the Colonies in North America, from the Discovery of the Country to the Year 1776. Collected by Peter Force. 4 vols. Washington, 1836, 1838, 1844, 1846.

Ford, Worthington Chauncey (compiler). List of the Vernon-Wager Manuscripts in the Library of Congress. Washington, 1904.

Gaffarel, Paul. Histoire de la Floride Française. Paris, 1875.

García, Genaro (editor). Dos Antiguas Relaciones de la Florida. Mexico, 1902.

Gentleman's Magazine and Historical Chronicles. Edited by Sylvanus Urban, Gentleman. 253 vols. London, 1731–1883.

Georgia. The Colonial Records of the State of Georgia. Atlanta, 1904–. (Abbreviated in the footnotes as Ga. Col. Rec).

Georgia Historical Society. Collections of the Georgia Historical Society. 9 vols. Savannah, 1840–1916.

Great Britain: Historical Manuscripts Commission. Fourteenth Report, Appendix, Part IX. The Manuscripts of the Earl of Buckinghamshire, The Earl of Lindsey, The Earl of Onslow, Lord Emly, Theodore J. Hare, Esq., and James Round, Esq., M.P. Presented to both Houses of Parliament by Command of Her Majesty. London, 1895. See *Hare* and *Trevor*.

Great Britain: Parliament. Papers Relative to the Rupture with Spain, Laid Before Both Houses of Parliament on Friday the Twenty-ninth Day of January, 1762, by His Majesty's Command. London, 1762.

Great Britain: Parliament. Cobbett's Parliamentary History of England. From the Norman Conquest, in 1066, to the Year 1803. From which Last-Mentioned Epoch it is Continued Downwards in the Work Entitled "Cobbett's Parliamentary Debates," etc. London, 1806–1924.

Great Britain: Privy Council. Acts of the Privy Council of England. Colonial Series, 1613–1783. 6 vols. Hereford, 1908–1912.

Great Britain: Public Record Office. Calendar of State Papers, Colonial Series, America and the West Indies. 1574–1709. 20 vols. London, 1860–1922.

GREENHOW, ROBERT. The History of Florida, Louisiana, Texas, and California, and of the Adjoining Countries, including the whole Valley of the Mississippi. From the Discovery to their Incorporation with the United States of America. New York, 1856.

HABERSHAM, HON. JAMES. The Letters of Hon. James Habersham, 1756–1775. In Collections of the Georgia Historical Society, Vol. VI. Savannah, 1904.

HARE, THEODORE J. Manuscripts of Theodore J. Hare, Esq., of Borden Wood, Hants. In the Fourteenth Report, Appendix, Part IX of Historical Manuscripts Commission. London, 1895.

HARING, CLARENCE HENRY. The Buccaneers in the West Indies in the XVII Century. New York, 1910.

HARRIS, F. R. Life of Edward Montagu, First Earl of Sandwich, 1625–1672. 2 vols. London, 1912.

HARRIS, JOHN. Navigantium atque Itinerantium Bibliotheca. Or, A Complete Collection of Voyages and Travels. Consisting of above Six hundred of the most Authentic Writers. 2 vols. London, 1744–1748.

HART, FRANCIS RUSSELL. Admirals of the Caribbean. Boston, 1922.

HERTSLET, LEWIS, ESQ. A Complete Collection of the Treaties and Conventions, and Reciprocal Regulations, at present subsisting between Great Britain and Foreign Powers, and of the Laws, Decrees, and Orders in Council, concerning the same; so far as They Relate to Commerce and Navigation; to the Repression and Abolition of the Slave Trade; and to the Privileges and Interests of the Subjects of the High Contracting Parties. 4 vols. London, 1840.

HERTZ, GERALD BERKELEY. British Imperialism in the Eighteenth Century. London, 1908.

HISTORICAL MAGAZINE, and Notes and Queries Concerning the Antiquities, History and Biography of America. 23 vols. Boston, 1857–1875.

HODGE, FREDERICK W., and LEWIS, THEODORE H. (editors). Spanish Explorers in the Southern United States, 1528–1543. New York, 1907.

JAMESON, JOHN FRANKLIN. Privateering and Piracy in the Colonial Period: Illustrative Documents. Edited Under the Auspices of the National Society of the Colonial Dames of America. New York, 1923.

JOHNSON, JAMES GUYTON. "The Spanish Period of Georgia and South Carolina, 1566–1702." In Bulletin of the University of Georgia. Athens, 1923.

JOHNSON, JAMES GUYTON. "The Yamassee Revolt of 1597 and the Destruction of the Georgia Missions." In Georgia Historical Quarterly, Vol. VII. Savannah, 1923.

JONES, CHARLES C., JR. The Dead Towns of Georgia. Savannah, 1878.

JONES, CHARLES C., JR. The History of Georgia. 2 vols. Boston, 1883.

LAUGHTON, J. K. "Jenkins' Ear." In English Historical Review, Vol. IV. London, 1889.

LEE, CHARLES, Attorney General of the United States (compiler). A Report of the Attorney General to Congress; Containing a Collection of Charters, Treaties, and Other Documents, Relative to and Explanatory of the Title to the Land Situate in the South Western Parts of the United States; and Claimed by Certain Companies Under a Law of the State of Georgia, Passed January 7, 1795. Printed by order of the Senate of the United States. Philadelphia, 1796.

LESCARBOT, MARC. Histoire de Novvelle-France. Paris, 1611.

LOWERY, WOODBURY. The Spanish Settlements Within the Present Limits of the United States, 1513–1561. New York, 1911.

LOWERY, WOODBURY. The Spanish Settlements Within the Present Limits of the United States. Florida, 1562–1574. New York, 1911.

M'CALL, CAPTAIN HUGH. The History of Georgia, Containing Brief Sketches of the Most Remarkable Events up to the Present Day (1784). Atlanta, 1909.

McCrady, Edward. The History of South Carolina under the Proprietary Government, 1670–1719. New York, 1897.

McCrady, Edward. The History of South Carolina under the Royal Government, 1719–1776. New York, 1899.

McCrady, Edward. The History of South Carolina in the Revolution, 1775–1780. New York, 1902.

MacDonald, William (editor). Select Charters and other Documents illustrative of American History, 1606–1773. New York, 1906.

Margry, Pierre (editor). Découvertes et Établissements des Français dans L'Ouest et Dans le Sud de L'Amérique Septentrionale (1614–1754). Mémoires et Documents Originaux recueillis et Publiés Par Pierre Margry. Paris, M Dccc Lxxxi.

Mereness, Newton D. (editor). Travels in the American Colonies. Edited Under the Auspices of the National Society of the Colonial Dames of America. New York, 1916.

Montiano, Don Manuel de. Letters addressed to Don Juan Francisco de Guemes y Horcasitas, Governor General of Cuba. Translation in Collections of the Georgia Historical Society, Vol. VII, Part I. Savannah, 1909.

Morley, John. Walpole. London, 1909.

North Carolina. The Colonial Records of North Carolina Published Under the Supervision of the Trustees of the Public Libraries, by Order of the General Assembly; Collected and Edited by William L. Saunders, Secretary of State. Raleigh, 1886–90.

Osgood, Herbert L. The American Colonies in the Eighteenth Century. 3 vols. New York, 1924.

Parkman, Francis. Pioneers of France in the New World. Boston, 1880.

Phillips, Philip Lee (editor). The Lowery Collection. A Descriptive List of Maps of the Spanish Possessions Within the Present Limits of the United States, 1502–1820. By Woodbury Lowery. Washington, 1912.

RIVERS, WILLIAM J. A Sketch of the History of South Carolina to the Close of the Proprietary Government by the Revolution of 1719. With an Appendix Containing Many Valuable Records Hitherto Unpublished. Charleston, 1856.

ROSS, MARY. "French Intrusions and Indian Uprisings in Georgia and South Carolina, 1577–1580." In Georgia Historical Quarterly, Vol. VII. Savannah, 1923.

ROSS, MARY. "The French on the Savannah, 1605." In Georgia Historical Quarterly, Vol. VIII. Savannah, 1924.

RUIDÍAZ Y CARAVIA, EUGENIO. La Florida su Conquista y Colonización por Pedro Menéndez de Avilés. 2 vols. Madrid, 1893. See *Connor*.

RUSSELL, LORD JOHN (editor). Correspondence of John, Fourth Duke of Bedford: Selected from the Originals at Woburn Abbey, with an Introduction. 3 vols. London, 1842, 1843, 1846.

SALLEY, ALEXANDER SAMUEL (editor). Journal of the Commons House of Assembly of South Carolina for the Session Beginning September 20, 1692, and Ending October 15, 1692. Columbia, 1907.

SALLEY, ALEXANDER SAMUEL (editor). Journals of the Commons House of Assembly of South Carolina for the Four Sessions of 1693. Columbia, 1907.

SALLEY, ALEXANDER SAMUEL (editor). Journal of the Commons House of Assembly of South Carolina, for the Session Beginning January 30, 1696, and Ending March 17, 1696. Columbia, 1908.

SALLEY, ALEXANDER SAMUEL (editor). Journal of the Grand Council of South Carolina, August 25, 1671–June 24, 1680; April 11, 1690–September 26, 1692. 2 vols. Columbia, 1907.

SCHÖNE, LUCIEN. La Politique Coloniale Sous Louis XV et Louis XVI. Paris, 1907.

SERRANO Y SANZ, MANUEL (editor). Documentos Históricos de La Florida y La Luisiana. Siglos XVI al XVIII. Biblioteca de los Americanistas. Madrid, 1912.

SHAFTESBURY, LORD. The Shaftesbury Papers and Other Records Relating to Carolina and the First Settlement on Ashley River Prior to the Year 1676. Published by the South Carolina Historical Society. Prepared for Publication by Langdon Cheves, Esq. In Collections of the South Carolina Historical Society, Vol. V. Charleston, 1897.

SHEA, JOHN GILMARY. History of the Catholic Church in the United States. 4 vols. New York, 1886–1892.

SHEPHERD, WILLIAM R. "The Cession of Louisiana to Spain." In Political Science Quarterly, September, 1904. Vol. XIX. New York, 1904.

SIMMS, WILLIAM GILMORE. The Yamassee: A Romance of Carolina. Chicago, 1890.

SMITH, WILLIAM ROY. South Carolina as a Royal Province, 1719–1776. New York, 1903.

SMOLLETT, TOBIAS GEORGE. Adventures of Roderick Random. London, n. d.

SMOLLETT, TOBIAS GEORGE, M.D. The History of England, from the Revolution in 1688 to the Death of George II. Designed as a Continuation of Hume. 6 vols. London, 1810, 1811.

SOLÍS DE MERÁS, DOCTOR GONZALO. Memorial que hizo el Doctor Gonzalo Solís de Merás, de todas las jornadas y sucesos del Adelantado Pedro Menéndez de Avilés, su cuñado, y de la Conquista de la Florida y Justicia que hizo en Juan Ribao y otros franceses. In Ruidíaz, op. cit.

SOUTH CAROLINA HISTORICAL SOCIETY. Collections of the South Carolina Historical Society. 5 vols. Charleston, 1857–1897.

SOUTH CAROLINA HISTORICAL AND GENEALOGICAL MAGAZINE. Charleston, 1900–.

STEVENS, REV. WILLIAM BACON, M.D. A History of Georgia from its First Discovery by Europeans to the Adoption of the present Constitution in MDCCXCVIII. 2 vols. New York, 1847.

STORER, MALCOLM. "Admiral Vernon Medals, 1739–1742."
In Proceedings of the Massachusetts Historical Society,
October, 1918–June, 1919. Boston, 1919.

SWANTON, JOHN R. Early History of the Creek Indians and
Their Neighbors. In the Bureau of American Ethnology,
Bulletin 73, Smithsonian Institution. Washington, 1922.

TEMPERLEY, HAROLD W. V. "The Causes of the War of
Jenkins' Ear, 1739." In Transactions of the Royal Historical Society. Third Series, Vol. III. London, 1909.

TEMPERLEY, HAROLD W. V. "The Relations of England with
Spanish-America, 1720–1744." In Annual Report of the
American Historical Association for the year 1911. Vol. I.
Washington, 1913.

TORQUEMADA, JUAN DE. Primera [segunda, tercera] parte de
los veinte i vn libros rituales i monarchía indiana, con el
origen y guerras, de los Indios Ocidentales, de sus poblaçones
descubrimiento, conquista, conuersion y otras cosas maraui-
llosas de la mesma tierra. Por F. Juan de Torquemada.
Madrid, 1723. Ed. by González de Barcía Carbillido y
Zuñiga.

TREVOR MANUSCRIPTS. See Buckinghamshire.

UNITED STATES. Sixtieth Congress, First Session, 1907–1908.
Senate Document Number 467. Boundary Line Between
Florida and Georgia. Certain Documents and Reports
Relating to the Locating and Marking of the Line Between
the Territory and State of Florida and the State of Georgia.
Presented by Mr. Bacon. Washington, 1908.

[VERNON, EDWARD]. An Account of the Expedition to Carthagena, with Explanatory Notes and Observations. Printed
for M. Cooper. London, 1743.

[VERNON, EDWARD]. Original Papers Relating to the Expedition to Carthagena. Printed for M. Cooper. London, 1744.

[VERNON, EDWARD]. Original Papers Relating to the Expedition to the Island of Cuba. Printed for M. Cooper. London, 1744.

[VERNON, EDWARD]. Original Papers Relating to the Expedition to Panama. Printed for M. Cooper. London, 1744.

WESLEY, REV. JOHN. The Journal of the Rev. John Wesley, A.M. Enlarged from Original Manuscripts, with Notes from Unpublished Diaries. Edited by Nehemiah Curnock. 8 vols. London, 1909–1916. See *Curnock*.

WINSOR, JUSTIN. Narrative and Critical History of America, Edited by Justin Winsor. 8 vols. Boston and New York, 1884–1889.

WRIGHT, IRENE A. "Spanish Policy toward Virginia." In American Historical Review, Vol. XXV. Washington, 1920.

WRIGHT, ROBERT. A Memoir of General James Oglethorpe, One of the Earliest Reformers of Prison Discipline in England, and the Founder of Georgia, in America. London, 1867.

YORKE, PHILIP C. The Life and Correspondence of Philip Yorke, Earl of Hardwicke, Lord High Chancellor of Great Britain. 3 vols. Cambridge, 1913.

INDEX

INDEX

132   INDEX

Segura, Juan Bautista, Jesuit Father, missionary at Axacan, Virginia, martyred, 11.
Seminoles, friendly to Spain, 68.
Seven Years' War, Spain enters, 15, 107–108.
Slaves, Indian, 34, 36.
Smith, John, 24.
Smuggling, English, 77.
Solís, Alonso, puts down rebellion in Guale, 12.
South Carolina, English Colony, 28–30; incites Guale Indians, 36, 39; Spain plans to invade, 93.
South Carolina region, Spanish pioneers in, 6–27; missions, 21.
South Sea Company, privileges of, 77; suspended, 82; terminated, 100.
Spain, enters Seven Years' War, 5; loses Florida, 5; regains influence over Apalaches, 63; protests Oglethorpe's regiment, 75; plans to re-annex Georgia, 75; military preparations, 75–76; suppresses English smuggling, 77; protests English war preparations, 78–9; prepares for war, 90, 92; campaign against Georgia, 94–96; demands Georgia, 99; conciliatory, 100; neutral in French War, 101; opposes New Hanover, 103, joins French War, 107; loses Florida, 107.
Spaniards, defeated on Flint River, 59; captives given up by Creeks, 64; alarmed at English advance, 69; settle on Cumberland Island, 104.
Spanish settlements, included in Carolina grant, 70.
Stephens, Thomas, criticises Trustees, 91; punished, 91.
Swanton, Dr. J. R., works cited, 29, 41, 48, 55, 59, 61, 67.
Talaje, town destroyed, 17; Fr. Pedro Delgado at mission, 19, 21.
Talapoosa, (Talapus), English expelled from, 66.
Tallahassee district (See *Apalache*), mission destroyed, 4.
Tama, friars visit, 15–16, 21; colony projected for, 18.
Tasquique, town, burned by Matheos, 51.
Teguale, Fernández meets Old Brimins at, 66.
Timucua missions, 25, 35.
Tolomato, mission, Fr. Corpa at, 15; uprising at, 16; Indian town destroyed, 17.
Torres, Admiral, protects Havana, 89, 92.
Torres, Governor Laureano de, sends campaign against Apalachicolas, 56; boundary dispute, 57.
Torres, Pedro de, expedition to interior, 25.
Traders, Carolina, in back country, 3.
Treaty of 1670, provisions discussed, 32, 70; Cabrera ordered to observe, 37; cited by both England and Spain, 98.
Treaty of 1748, 100.
Treaty of 1750, 100.
Treaty of 1763, 108.

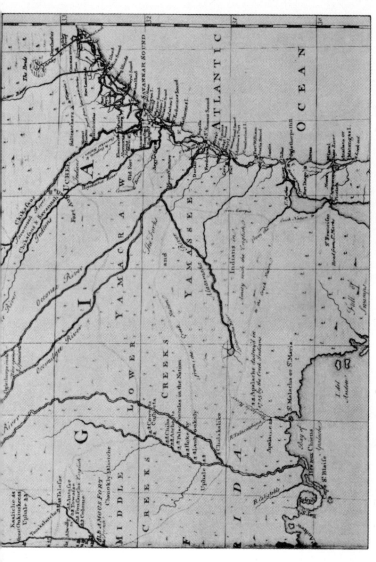

Bowen's map of the Georgia country, 1748.   From Harris, *Voyages and Travels*, vol. II.